Chuck and Gladys Dart

Manley Hot Springs

Chuck and Gladys Dart

Manley Hot Springs

SPIRIT MOUNTAIN PRESS

ISBN: 0-910871-07-8

Interviewing and Editing:
Yvonne Yarber and Curt Madison

Photography:
Curt Madison (unless otherwise noted)

Material collected October 1978 and March 1979
in Manley Hot Springs and Ruby, Alaska

Manuscript approved by Chuck and Gladys Dart in 1982.

SPIRIT MOUNTAIN PRESS
P.O. BOX 1214 FAIRBANKS, ALASKA 99707

Produced and funded by:
Yukon-Koyukuk School District of Alaska

Regional School Board:
Donald Honea Sr. - Chairman
Pat McCarty - Vice Chairman
Eddie Bergman - Treasurer
Fred Lee Bifelt - Clerk
Luke Titus

Superintendent: Joe Cooper
Assistant Superintendent: Fred Lau
Project Coordinator: Don Kratzer

Supplemental funding:
Johnson O'Malley Grant - EOOC14202516

**Library of Congress
Cataloging in Publication Data**

Madison, Curt
Yarber, Yvonne
Dart, Chuck and Gladys - Manley Hot
Springs. A Biography.
YKSD Biography Series
ISBN 0-910871-07-8

1. Dart, Chuck and Gladys 2. Manley Hot
Springs 3. Alaska Biography

Cover photo:
Chuck and Gladys in their hot springs home, 1984.

Frontispiece:
Gladys Dart, Diane Dart, Grandma Edna Reed and Chuck Dart in front of the Dart's home in Manley Hot Springs, 1982.

Foreword

This book is the fifteenth produced by the Yukon-Koyukuk School District in a series meant to provide cultural understanding of our own area and relevant role models for students. Too often Interior Alaska is ignored in books or mentioned only in conjunction with its mineral resources such as the gold rush or oil pipeline. We are gauged by what we are worth to Outside people. People living in the Interior certainly have been affected by those things but also by missionaries, wage labor, fur prices, celebrations, spring hunts, schools, technology, potlatches, and much more. For residents, Interior Alaska is all of those things people do together, whether in the woods, on the river, in the village or on Two Street. It's a rich and varied culture often glossed over in favor of things more easily written and understood.

This project was begun in 1977 by Bob Maguire. Representatives of Indian Education Parent Committees from each of Yukon-Koyukuk School District's eleven villages met in Fairbanks February of 1978 to choose two people from each village to write about. A variety of selection means were used—from school committees to village council elections. Despite the fact that most of the representatives were women, few women were chosen for the books. As the years passed, more women were added to give a more complete accounting of recent cultural changes.

It is our goal to provide a vehicle for people who live around us so they can describe the events of their lives in their own words. To be singled out as an individual as we have done in this series has not always been comfortable for the biographees, particularly for those who carry the strong Koyukon value of being humble. Talking about oneself has been a conflict overridden by the desire and overwhelming need to give young people some understanding of their own history in a form they have become accustomed to. A growing number of elders who can't read or write themselves think young people won't believe anything unless it's written in a book. This project attempts to give oral knowledge equal time in the schools.

As materials of this kind become more common, methods of gathering and presenting oral history get better. The most important ingredient is trust. After many hours of interview, people often relax to the point of saying some personal things they prefer left unpublished. After editing the tape transcripts we bring the rough draft manuscript back to the biographees to let them add or delete things before it becomes public. Too often those of us living in rural Alaska have been researched *on* or written *about* for an audience far away. This series is meant to bring information full round--from us back to us for our own uses.

Too many people in the Interior have felt ripped-off by journalists and bureaucrats. Hundreds pass through every year, all wanting information and many never to return. Occasionally their finished work may find its way back to the source only to flare emotions when people feel misrepresented. Perhaps a tight deadline or the lack of travel money may be the excuse for not returning for verification or approval. That is no consolation for people who opened up and shared something of themselves and are left feeling betrayed. We work closely with the biographees to check facts and intentions. The books need to be intimate and daring but the last thing we want to do is make someone's life more difficult. We need to share information in a wholesome way. After all, we're all in this together.

Comments about the biographies, their use, corrections, questions, or anything else is welcome.

Curt Madison
Yvonne Yarber
December 10, 1982
Manley Hot Springs
Alaska 99756

Acknowledgements

Many people have helped with this book. Irene Reed, Gladys' sister in Fairbanks gave Finnish spellings and translations, family tree information and logistical support. Her mother, Grandma Reed, also provided family tree information and savory Finnish bread. Our neighbors in Manley Hot Springs gave life, color and friendship. Cheryl DeHart typed transcripts and the final manuscript. Janis Carney and Liza Vernet donated proofreading talents. Bob Maguire's idea began the series. Dona Sieden of the Minnesota Historical Society and Renee Blahuta of the University of Alaska Archives helped with archive photos. Fred Lau, Mavis Brown and Joe Cooper have given administrative support while the Yukon-Koyukuk Regional School Board provided money and an interest in local curriculum. The staff of Spirit Mountain Press brought this book into final print: Larry Laraby owner and manager, Doug Miller graphic artist and Eva Bee the indispensable typesetter.

Thank you.

All royalties from the sale of this book go to the Yukon-Koyukuk School District for the production of more autobiographies.

This is the first printing of this book. Please let us know about any corrections for future printings.

Table Of Contents

Glossary

acrid - sharp of bitter to the taste or smell

antipathy - strong aversion or dislike, disgust

avarice - insatiable desire for wealth; greedy

bootleg - to illegally make, sell or transport goods such as liquor; word originated with the practice of concealing objects in the leg of a high boot

catalyst - a subtance which either speeds up or slows down a chemical reaction, but which itself undergoes no permanent chemical change

ego - one's sense of importance; self esteem

Gisakk **-** the Koyukon Athabaskan version of a Pan-Alaska term for White man, comes from the Russian word *kazak* which is translated in English as cossack. The Central Yupik version of this word is *kass'aq*

mecca - place that many people visit or yearn to go to; originates from the city of Mecca, Saudi Arabia, a holy place to which many Moslems make pilgrimages

moonshine - whiskey or other alcoholic beverage smuggled or made illegally

ostensibly - apparent, evident

Pet 4 - National Petroleum Reserve No. 4; it covers Barrow and much of the North Slope

sauna - Finnish dry-heat sweat bath where bathers produce steam by throwing water on hot stones

sedge - any of a large family (Cyperaceae) of grasslike herbs growing in damp places

victrola - a phonograph; a trademark of an early phonograph

Local Area:

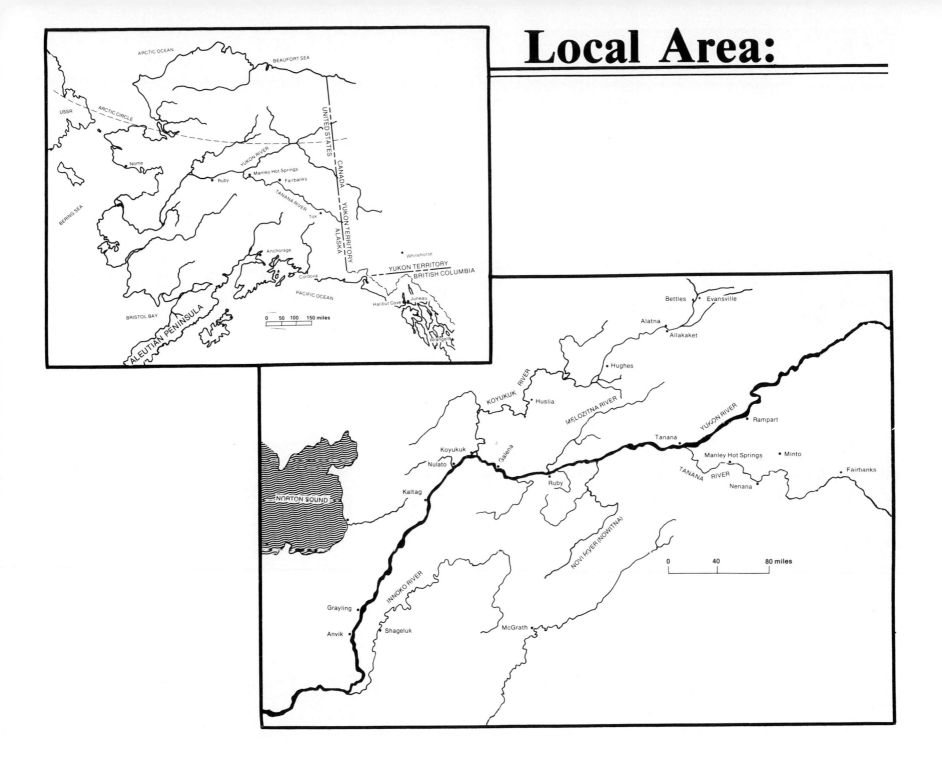

East-side view of bathhouse, storage shed and Dart cabin used as a school in the 50's.

Cy Hetherington and Chuck Dart, 1983.

Introduction

Gladys and Chuck Dart live in the village of Manley Hot Springs on the Tanana River. The town is situated on the edge of Koyukon and Tanana Athabaskan language areas and was traditionally used by both nomadic groups. The Koyukon name for the hot springs area is *Toonaali*Ⅰ *Dinh* or "place where the water is hot".

The early 1900's brought many newcomers who first named the settlement Baker Hot Springs and soon after just Hot Springs. It was a gold rush boom town supply center with a newspaper, federal marshal, mining district recorder's office and a larger population than Fairbanks. In 1957 or '58 the name was changed to Manley Hot Springs after an early resident because too much mail was missent to Hot Springs, Arkansas. Since it's early years as Hot Springs, Manley Hot Springs has become a small village with few jobs and a winter population of sixty to eighty people. It is a Native village under the Alaska Native Land Claims Act although the population is predominately non-Native.

Photo by Yvonne Yarber

As the name suggests, there are active hot springs, a major feature of the village and the lives of Chuck and Gladys who own them. The hot springs provide warm fertile ground for the Dart's large greenhouses and outdoor gardens. At the same time they bring a continual flow of visitors seeking a hot bath in the simple bathhouse. The Dart's hospitality is to be marvelled for you never know who might answer their door on a summer day. Their guests come from such faraway places as Japan, Germany, Africa and Switzerland.

Despite many summer tourists the Darts have chosen not to develop the springs into a large scale resort area. Instead they maintain a small family business geared more towards community residents than visitors. The Dart's greenhouse produces hundreds of pounds of tomatoes each summer season as well as eggplant, melons, bellpeppers and cucumbers.

Gladys Dart was the first teacher in the reorganized Manley Hot Springs grade school in 1958. She continues to teach half of the school year in the multigrade one-room school with her famous balance of discipline and affection.

Together as immigrants to Alaska, Chuck and Gladys' story is another facet of life in the Interior.

Chuck and Gladys during spring planting in their greenhouse 1983.

11

Chapter One: Chuck's Childhood

A Railroad Town

My grandfather was a stone mason. He had immigrated from Scotland to Minnesota and set up at a granite quarry on the outskirts of St. Cloud, Minnesota, about 120 miles from Proctor. He had blank tombstones as well as building blocks stacked up alongside his house so when I went to visit it was like going to a cemetery. Also within sight of the house was a big reformatory built in the old style with high granite walls and turrets on top. It looked like a strange castle and I had fantasies of break outs and being kidnapped.

But we didn't really know too much about our past. As kids, frankly, we weren't much interested. I'm ashamed to say but when my mother started talking about the past I got pretty turned off. Now I'd really like to know about things.

Christmastime both of my grandmothers would send us cookies and gifts. My father's mother lived in Ohio and she would send dried corn, dried apples, and sugar cookies. My mother's mother in Minnesota sent cakes, shortbread and gifts for the kids. We could eat the food right away, but we had to save the gifts until Christmas morning.

I was born February 5, 1922, in Proctor, Minnesota. It's a suburb of Duluth and essentially it's a big railroad yard. Iron ore was brought in by train from the Mesabi Range, sorted and sent to Duluth to be shipped to the steel mills. Proctor was a company town. About ninety percent of the men worked for the railroad.

It was a good place for a kid to grow up. Behind the row of houses across our street was a pasture and beyond that the woods. We had a creek not far away that we could raft in summer and skate on in the winter. That creek

A steam shovel drops eighty tons of iron ore into a fifty ton bottom-dump steel car at the Burt-Day-Sellers open pit iron mine at Hibbing, Minnesota, circa 1935.

Traffic gate at the St. Cloud Reformatory, Minnesota circa 1925.

went through the Duluth Zoo and one time a couple seals escaped and swam up the creek. We watched them swim around in a reservoir until the Zoo people came and recaptured them.

Once the cold damp winds off Lake Superior blew in a sleet storm so severe the ice piled on the power lines snapped them off and we were out of school for a week. The whole area was covered with a heavy crust of ice, rougher than glare ice but not so bad you couldn't put skates on and go all over town, even into the woods. That storm iced up a railroad switch and derailed a train too. I remember skating around the cars.

My father was a railroad man. He was a conductor on one of the iron ore trains. The line wasn't long. It just went to the iron mines and a few other small towns, but it had the biggest steam locomotives in the world. Sixteen drive-wheels, and trains more than a mile long loaded with ore. You could hear them chugging up the grade from Duluth a long ways off and smell the acrid smoke of their coal burners. Sometimes kids would jump on the ore cars and ride a ways before jumping off. But that was dangerous and one kid lost a leg by doing that.

I never rode on an ore train when my father was conductor, but we had passes to passenger trains all over the States, Mexico and Canada because of his job. I took a couple long trips on those passes, but usually we'd hop on the train and just go to a swimming hole about forty miles away. We'd take a can of beans for lunch, a knife to open the can, and a spoon.

A creek came near the train station both in Alborne and Silica so we'd get off at one of them. After swimming we'd cook our lunch and head home. Sometimes we'd hang our heads out the window and get cinders in our hair.

Duluth Massabe & Iron Range 110 foot long "Big Boy", the largest locomotive ever built.

Trains were very important to people then and I'm still addicted to them. I have an inner feeling for the mystique of trains that I don't have for other forms of transportation.

Working conditions on the railroads were pretty bad in the early days. In fact, it was so common for men to lose fingers coupling cars that when they were hiring men everyone had to raise their hands. Those men missing fingers were hired because it proved they had experience. By the time I came along the Unions were well established and conditions were better.

My father was involved in politics and the Union for a long time. He was president of the local Brotherhood of Railroad Trainmen and a lobbyist to the State legislature. I guess some of his interest in politics spun off on me.

He was active in the Farmer-Labor Party which was the Progressive Party in Minnesota. The other major party at the time was the Republican Party and my mother belonged to it. She was more conservative than he was. Frequently my mother would be a delegate to the Republican Party at the same time my father was a delegate to the Farmer-Labor Party. So I got it at home from both sides.

My father was appointed Clerk of the Public Domain under Governor Benson and was in charge of State lands, much like the Secretary of the Interior is in charge of Federal lands. He had to be in St. Paul for the legislature, but it was only about two or three months, not six months like in Alaska now.

For twelve years he was an elected Municipal Judge in Proctor. I don't know much about his courtroom situation. I was pretty young then. He handled local ordinances and he could marry people, but not divorce them. I enjoyed the place he worked. As a little kid I had the run of the courtroom, jail, and fire station. I used to like to go see the two big red shiny fire engines.

John Graham was the one-man police department of Proctor, but he had the title Chief of Police. He was a big man, a little overweight and impressive. Once I was running in and out of the jail cells and he closed the door on me. He told me I was going to be locked up for a long time. Really gave me the business. I knew then I never wanted to be behind bars.

Proctor City Hall circa 1940.

Proctor's fire engine circa 1930.

My mother had been a school teacher before she married my father. After that besides being a housewife she tried her hand at a few businesses. It was her idea to raise chickens and to this day I don't like chickens, live ones anyway. When I was in high school she and another lady in town opened a knitting shop. She enjoyed knitting and teaching other women to knit. The shop didn't make much money, but I'm sure it made a little.

Depression days nobody had much money. Railroad work was seasonal because the ore ships could only travel when the ice left Lake Superior. And since the steel mills weren't making much steel, there wasn't much ore to haul. Only the railroad men with the most seniority got to work. As far as being in poverty, I was not aware of it. Everybody was in the same boat. Little kids pretty much adapt to the situation they find themselves in anyway. They don't have any standard of comparison. Their form of life is the only thing they know so it's no big thing. We didn't go without food, but it was probably more or less a continuing source of concern for my parents like it was for virtually everyone there.

We had a garden and, for a while, chickens, but they didn't contribute a real significant amount to the food budget. We got most of our food at the store. I remember my mother saying, "Go to the store and get a fifteen cent soup bone." You got a pretty big bone for fifteen cents. She made vegetable beef soup and it was really good. I wish I knew how she did it. Barley, potatoes, carrots, rutabagas, and I don't know what all. She tried to teach my brother and I to cook saying, "It won't hurt you to learn." But we wouldn't do it.

I have two older brothers and a sister. I am the youngest. The younger brother was eighteen months older than me and quite a bit bigger and stronger. It seemed like he used to beat me up everyday just to keep in practice. I never learned. Somehow he would get me to taunt him and then he'd have an excuse to work me over.

Begin School

I was in love with my kindergarten teacher, Viola Lundberg. As a matter of fact, I had a crush on most of my teachers. First grade was Irma Rust and I liked her. The second grade teacher didn't like me much and the feeling was mutual. I really felt cheated when she moved up to fifth grade and I caught her there again. Third grade was Rose Glenn. I liked her a lot. Fourth grade was Mabel Henwood and I was in love with her, too.

Sixth grade class of Proctor Summit School 1933. Chuck Dart is front and center with overalls and bow-tie.

The school was a fairly large brick building. Every morning before we went into the classroom we lined up in the halls. Then the janitor played the Washington Post March on the victrola and we marched into the classroom. No one would do anything like that anymore, but I really liked it.

Our seats were alphabetical in every class right through high school. That means that I sat next to the same kids all the time I was in school. The only way it changed was if you got into trouble and had to be moved to another seat.

I can't think of anything in the academic line that I was particularly indebted to any one teacher for. I was really no-great-shakes as a student. I was more for enjoying life while I was there.

At home all of us kids had chores to do. We had to get wood in for the kitchen stove and the heater. Much of the time we burned coal in the heater, but whatever it was we had to get it in. And I had to do dishes. My brother and I would squabble about whose turn it was to wash or dry. We had to take care of the doggone chickens and pull weeds for them. I hated chickens then and I haven't gotten to like them much yet.

Our water came from Lake Superior. It was really good water, cold, clear and soft. A few years ago we found out that it was polluted. A mill crushing iron ore was putting asbestos fibers into the lake. And now people can't drink it without risking danger from the asbestos. Developing the iron ore industry gave a lot of people jobs, but it spoiled the drinking water. It is important to be careful about things like that.

Tag

We had a lot of tag games that we played at night. One of them, we used a power pole for a goal. Somebody would be "it" and the rest would go hide. The guy that was "it" would have to find the others and then beat them back to the goal. You had to get them all out before the game was over. If a person beat you back to the goal all the ones you already got would be freed.

Then there was a game our parents wouldn't let us play. We used clubs and cans. I guess too often kids got clubbed instead of cans. There would be two cans set up as a goal on one end of the alley and two on the other end. One can was set right in the middle. It started out like hockey. One guy from each team would "face off" over the center can. Once the can was in play, we all went after it, clubs whacking away as hard as they could. Kids got hit on the legs or God knows where. All our clubs were sturdy sticks too. We had pick handles or good stout branches out of the woods. It's surprising we got by as long as we did without someone getting really damaged.

Rhubarb and Saturday Evening Post

We didn't have much in the way of money, but a kid didn't need much. Baby Ruth candy bars weighed in at a quarter pound for a nickel. We sold rhubarb to some ladies in the neighborhood for four cents a pound. It wasn't long before you saturated the neighborhood though so we had some other schemes too. One old lady, I don't know how old she was — anyone past thirty was old, was really an easy touch. We'd pick her some wild flowers or something and she'd always have a few pennies or some candy for us.

I sold magazines door to door — *Liberty, Saturday Evening Post,* and *Collier's.* You could only sell one kind at a time because the agents handling them were in competition. Asking price was a nickel and I got 1¼ cent out of that. I think I sold more than the other kids in the neighborhood because I really got out there and knocked on every door.

Rub Don't Blot Cigarettes

My mother threatened to spank us a lot more than she actually did. When my brother and I were fighting in another room, she'd call out for us to stop. Usually we didn't and usually she came in and spanked both of us to be sure to get the one that caused the trouble.

Cigarette smoking was a crime at our house. Sometimes we got an older kid to buy us a pack of *Wings* or *Twenty Grands* for a dime, but usually we rolled our own. There was a paper towel dispenser in the train depot that was stamped "Rub Don't Blot" so that was the name of our cigarettes — *Rub Don't Blot* Cigarettes. My mother was a string saver and we would mooch some of her string out of a jar for the "tobacco." We'd roll it up in the paper towel darn near as big as a cigar and just spit on the paper towel to hold it together. Pretty evil but somehow we managed to smoke it.

The last spanking I got was over smoking. I was thirteen and came home half-sick from having smoked a cigar. My mother was really mad because she talked to us about smoking a number of times. That time she took a shoe and really whaled my hind end. Between being half-sick, the spanking, and not enjoying smoking that much anyway, I decided it wasn't worth it. I never did smoke too much after that.

Treat Everyone Well

There were some drunks in our neighborhood we would see and follow around. Sometimes we would taunt them but usually not because they could be real generous, maybe give us a nickel or quarter. It wasn't often though that we saw a man obviously drunk. When I was a small kid it was still Prohibition. The repeal of the Prohibition Act coincided with the inauguration of Roosevelt in 1933.

Proctor had a liquor store after the repeal but the people voted to close it down and put in a city-run liquor store instead. There was quite a bit of opposition to that by some people. They felt it was socialist and they were being dictated to. One guy, nicknamed Romeo, was particularly against it. He was a pretty heavy boozer, but he said he would never buy from a city-run store. Very shortly after the old store closed and the new one opened, I guess he felt a dire need for some booze. He disguised himself to go in and buy some. He made his face black by putting burnt cork on it. He wanted to look like a Black man so no one would guess it was Romeo going into the liquor store. Well, there was only one Black in the community so it wasn't much of a disguise.

The Black guy was a janitor at the bank and also a shoeshine man. I don't know whose shoes he shined. Certainly nobody in our family had that kind of money to squander on a shoeshine.

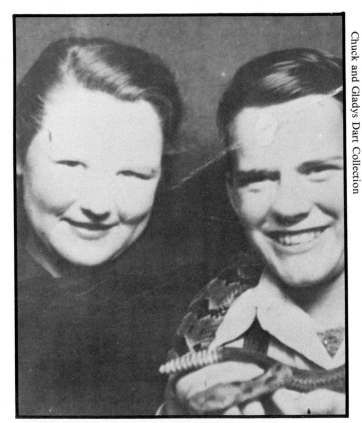

Chuck and Gladys Dart Collection

Mary Peterson and Chuck Dart circa 1937.

Tom was a real nice guy. I don't know what his full name was, but us kids liked talking to him.

As far as I knew there wasn't prejudice towards Tom. There were people in Proctor who spoke about Blacks in a derogatory way. Using the word "nigger" was a common appellation. But in my own family, my father and mother were very outspoken about treating everyone well. We were not to make derogatory remarks about other people because of their race or physical condition. I remember my father talking to me about never hurting anybody's feeling about their mental condition either, like if they were crazy. He said, "You wouldn't poke fun at somebody that had a crippled body. You shouldn't poke fun at somebody that has a crippled mind."

Children and adults enjoying a Minnesota skating rink.

Photo by Bruce Sifford Studio, Minnesota Historical Society

Chapter Two: Chuck On His Own

Leaving the Country

Actually it was my sister who convinced me to go on to school, to college. Probably less than twenty-five percent of my high school class went to college and I might not have either but my sister gave me quite a pep talk about furthering my education and all. So for the first year I lived with my sister and her husband in Downsville, Wisconsin and went to Stout Institute. It was an uneventful year. I was never a great student, just a coaster. I could sit in a class, listen to a lecture, and pass without too much difficulty. But I was never one to dig things out and I was poor at writing papers or submitting things.

My parents paid for the first year, but I decided to pay my own way after that. I got a job as a stock boy in a dime store in Madison, Wisconsin. Pay was thirty cents an hour and my room and board came out of it so I didn't save much. In December my mother offered to take me on a long train trip south through Hot Springs, Arkansas to Mexico, up to California and Canada, then back to Duluth. We were still riding on railroad passes but she said it was the last trip she could give me. I was soon to be 21 and would no longer be eligible for passes. The trip sounded pretty good so I quit the dime store and went with her.

Fort St. John, British Columbia, July 1942. L-R: unidentified, Nick Swaab, 20 year old Chuck Dart.

We started the trip just after Pearl Harbor was bombed by the Japanese beginning World War II in the Pacific. The first stop was in Hot Springs, Arkansas. I'm sure that was the beginning of my interest in hot springs. My mother had arthritis so our stop there was medicinal.

The town had little fountains with hot springs water bubbling out of them and people walked around with little collapsible metal cups in their pockets. They would drink this stuff. It smelled and tasted awful. I didn't see how it was any good.

Along one street of town was a string of well constructed bathhouses called "Bathhouse Row." I don't know why but I never did take a hot springs bath while I was there. No interest I guess. At the time I was just unaware of the sensuous qualities of hot springs baths. Anyway, it was the first time I had seen lizards in the wild. I caught some of them in the park. It was a matter of taking a little stick with a string, making a noose and quickly slipping it over the head of the lizard. If you moved slowly you could do it.

We went on to San Antonio and Mexico City. I enjoyed both places, but by the time we got back to San Antonio I had spent the money I saved to go to school so I left my mother and came back to Proctor.

The war was on and a lot of people were getting drafted or enlisting in the service. It was the thing to do. I tried to enlist in the Marines in San Antonio but they turned me down flat. They wouldn't take anyone with glasses. Really punctured my ego.

Back in Proctor a high school friend told me about a chance to go work building the Alaska Highway. A little outfit in Minnesota, Standard Salt and Cement, had the contract to clear the right-of-way. We went down and applied but the War Manpower Board had to approve anyone leaving the country. Danny couldn't go so I went alone. I was not quite 21.

Work on the Alaska Highway

I was a small kid when I first heard about Alaska. My father had a cousin who lived in Wrangell before World War I. In the family photo album we had pictures of totem poles and stuff. Also my father worked in northern

British Columbia before World War I on a railroad called the Edmonton, Dunvagen, and British Columbia. He liked it very much. His plan was to come to Alaska to live when he retired. I guess I was pretty well primed about Alaska before the highway job came up.

When I came north I signed a contract for thirty-five dollars a week plus room and board. In contrast with my job as a stock boy it was like heaven here. I couldn't work hard enough to earn such big money. My wages were raised to fifty dollars a week before the first week was out. It was absolutely hopeless to earn that kind of money at home. The room wasn't much, but the grub was great. I remember eating all the pineapple I wanted.

The contract had no stipulation about the number of hours a day so they worked me as much as they wanted. We got up at 4:30 to get breakfast ready for the crew. Then I'd do kitchen flunky jobs all day and not get finished until eight o'clock at night. Most of us were young kids working in the mess hall so we had a lot of energy to fool around. We'd go down to the Peace River and swim in the backwater. It was my first experience with the long sunny days and very short nights. We didn't have sense enough to go to bed so I was perpetually short of sleep for quite a while.

I wouldn't say I loved the work, but it was a big contrast to me and the atmosphere made it interesting. Stories drifted around the barracks. I was dumb and green and everything was interesting. Now I'd find it a nuisance. Some guy stumbling around in the middle of the night or sitting on the end of a bunk talking with a friend. After the job finished, I went back to Minnesota, then came north again to Whitehorse.

Chuck Dart above the Peace River near Fort St. John, July 1942.

Refinery

I got a job in an oil refinery near Whitehorse run by Bechtel, the same company that worked on the Trans-Alaska Pipeline. The process in the refinery was experimental and a high priority in the war effort. It was also risk.

First I was flunky in the kitchen, then a grease monkey in the Alkalations Section of the refinery. I took care of some valves on pipes running the catalyst, hydrofluoric acid.

Hydrofluoric acid is an extremely active acid. It dissolves glass and concrete. We had to wear special overalls, boots, gloves and hats with plastic face masks. Every eight hours we put live steam on the valves and pumped more lubricant into them. I don't know what it was but it was foul smelling.

One time there was a chamber, or tank, being opened for cleaning. It had been flushed out as much as possible and vented. The workman inside had a waterproof suit on. He accidentally dropped a nut into the sludge in the bottom of the tank. Then he made a mistake. He took his glove off to reach in and pick up the nut. Before the action of the acid could be stopped it had penetrated his flesh and dissolved the bones of his fingers to pencil-point fineness. Despite all our caution and safety measures, it was still a risky place to work.

I worked there for two years until the shut-down order came. We never did get into full production and I'm sure we never produced enough high octane gasoline to fuel the aircraft that supplied us with parts and material.

When we weren't working we had a little time to explore around. There were lake trout in a large deep lake outside Whitehorse Rapids. Wintertime we skied. I remember being quite interested in the country. I ordered books on Alaska and Yukon Territories. I even started a course on geology in the north and had several conversations with the editor of the Whitehorse newspaper about the Northland. I don't know how many people were interested that way. Even now it is not uncommon for Outside construction workers in Alaska to not know things about Alaska. Even obvious things like where the Tanana River is or the difference between Indians and Eskimos.

Amchitka

The war was still on when the refinery shut down. We were all still subject to the War Manpower Act so we couldn't change jobs or change employers without permission. I had the choice to go to Arabia or Amchitka. My roommate chose Arabia and I went to the Aleutian Islands. Amchitka was quite different from Whitehorse but beautiful. The sedges and grasses were very green.

I didn't travel the full length of the island, just the one end where the military installations were. The world's largest colony of sea otters

Chuck and Gladys Dart Collection

Whitehorse circa 1943.

Chuck and Gladys Dart Collection

Chuck Dart 1944.

is on Amchitka and blue foxes followed you around on the beach. There were quite a few water fowl and eagles. My memory may be tricking me on the eagles. It doesn't seem like they should be there, but I think they were. The island, of course, is volcanic and some of the lava formations were really interesting. One was called "pillow lava." It was extruded beneath the sea and when the land rose out of the water it became exposed.

I was a warehouseman which meant I issued lumber and parts to the various companies that were building the bases. But in my time most of the work was already done so much of the time I wasn't doing anything productive.

Most of the people there were from Outside although there was one crew from Alaska. I remember meeting a man from Halibut Cove and a couple Tlingit Indians. All of the Aleuts had been removed from the islands to somewhere else by the government.

I was on Amchitka when the war ended. I wanted to stay in Alaska and I wanted to go on to college. There was only one choice so I headed for Fairbanks.

Chuck at Amchitka, summer 1945.

College

The trip from Amchitka to Anchorage was something. I took a freight service boat to Adak and then waited a couple weeks for another boat to go to Whittier. Just out of Adak we ran into a bad storm on the Bering Sea. It was just like in the movies with the wind making the ropes sing in the rigging and waves breaking over the deck. Pitching around up and down quite a few got seasick, even the crew. When we landed at Dutch Harbor an ambulance came out to meet the ship and took off four guys that had been throwing up blood.

When I first came north I intended to save money to buy a farm in Wisconsin, but pretty soon I was just saving money. By the time I started

Chuck at the University of Alaska, Fairbanks 1948.

school at the University I had about $5,000, which was a pretty healthy stake at the time.

I was 23 and I thought I was going to be an old man, you know, coming to school at such an advanced age, but there were quite a few veterans in school older than I was. My purposes were not too well defined. I studied geology and biology mainly, but I also had courses in Alaska history, Alaska archaeology, and some anthropology.

I don't remember how much I budgeted for the first year of school, but it was all gone by Christmas with all the partying that was going on. We'd catch the bus into Fairbanks and go to the bar. The Rose Room was the best. Right on Second Avenue. The whole area between the Federal Building and Co-op Drug Store used to be wooden false-front structures. But that first winter they all burned down in a spectacular fire you could see from College Hill.

After the fire, the theater got turned into the Co-op Drug Store and the Rose Room was rebuilt into the Mecca Bar. Then it became the "mecca" of the college kids.

We had a ski club and we used to ski from Science Ridge, it was just a pasture then, down to the railroad tracks. We did a little cross-country skiing too, and some hunting. I can remember going up the Steese Highway after caribou. There were lots of caribou but I never got close enough to shoot one.

I went to the University off and on from the fall of '45 to the spring of '51. If I decided I wanted to take off and go prospecting or go to work or whatever, I'd drop out and do that.

Ladue Country

Warren Martin, Jack Finwey and I got together at school and decided we were going to go over to the Ladue country and discover gold. We took the

Chuck Dart holding two geese by the Ladue River, June 1946.

bus to Tok, then walked over the divide to the Dennison Forks between the Dennison and Ladue Rivers. That was our first experience with a niggerhead swamp and it was a dandy. Falling on those tussocks. You can't walk on them and you can't walk between them. You fall, pitch forward, and your pack rides up high as it can on your back, then you have a heck of a time getting on your feet again. It was spring, late May, and there was water over ice between those hummocks or tussocks, or whatever you want to call them. Really slippery.

One night it was heavy, overcast and fairly dark. Late May so the sky was light but it was comparatively dark. We got lost in the fog so we decided to stop and make camp. We didn't have a tent, just a tarp to pitch over the sleeping bags to keep the rain off. I had gotten in my bag and the other two were standing by the fire talking. Suddenly one of them yelled, "Bear!"

I sat up in my sleeping bag and said, "You can't shit me." But they didn't pay any attention. Both of them dived in there going for the guns. I looked out the open end of the tarp and there was a black bear coming right for us on a run. I have absolutely no memory of the time between seeing the bear and standing next to the other two shooting. My mind is a total blank. I guess I was so scared I just blacked it out. Martin had a .30-06. The first shot the bear spun sideways, silhouetted. Then he shot four more times. The second shot dropped the bear.

That bear puzzled us greatly. It went against all bear lore we had heard. Here we had a fire going, talking, making noise, and this bear comes charging at us. The only thing we could figure was that something had frightened it from behind, maybe a grizzly, but I don't know. That's the only thing that we could come up with.

We didn't last too much longer after the bear, maybe two or three days and we headed back. Martin was going up to Pet 4 to work. He decided he needed the money.

A few days after we got back to Fairbanks, I was in the Model Cafe with Fred Schikora and said, "Gee, I wish I was back in Ladue."

"Do you mean it?" he asked.

"Yeah," I said.

"Well, let's go."

We packed up and went back again. I learned on the first trip not to carry too much junk so we went light. Unfortunately, we cut the food supply short, too. We ate quite a few squirrels and a family of screech owls, the whole crew. The big ones weren't too big and the little ones were really small. All we got was one meal and I used to say even the gravy was tough.

We had a raven too, which was good eating. It was pretty much white meat, but really scrawny. And we had a porcupine. We hadn't run out of food, we just didn't have any meat. There wasn't much in the way of dried food then like there is now.

The trip was a week or ten days but we didn't find a thing. I don't think we even panned. We just hiked around. We built a raft on the Ladue River but the river at that time was too shallow and we ran into a lot of gravel bars so we gave it up and walked back. It took a couple days to walk out.

Gisakk

The first contact I had with Native people was at the University except for those two guys from Southeastern on Amchitka. I remember one of them, a young man, borrowed some money from me. Later when he saw me in Fairbanks, he paid me back. I was really impressed because that didn't always happen with White guys I'd lent money to. Since then I've gotten to know a lot of Native people.

It doesn't really bother me much when a Native calls me *Gisakk* when I'm the object of anti-White feelings or the expression of those feelings. I don't feel they are directing their antipathy towards me as Chuck Dart, but as "White man." And considering all the harsh things that have been said and done to Natives, Blacks and other minorities, I can understand where they're coming from and it doesn't bother me as much as it might if I didn't know this. In fact, its amazing to me that more minority people aren't bitterly and actively expressing themselves towards members of the White race for what we have done ever since Columbus set foot in the New World. So although I'm sorry that these things have accumulated and that there are some individuals that feel they must express this hatred and bitterness, I can certainly understand it. I don't like it and I regret that it occurs, but I can also be very sympathetic with the person expressing their feelings. However, I can be more sympathetic towards that person if the feelings are directed at someone else besides me.

There could be more constructive outlets for those feelings than angry words, but just the emotional release can be constructive too. Hopefully as people go through life anger will lessen rather than increase and there will be greater understanding.

Right now there is more freedom to express feelings of antagonism and bitterness than there has been earlier. Feelings have always been there, but the freedom to express them is relatively recent.

Politics

Politics are important to all of us and have a tremendous influence on so many aspects of our lives. There isn't much that isn't affected by politics. Indeed, many of the things we think of as being removed from politics are very political. Anytime there is taxation and expenditure of public funds it is certainly political. If you want to limit the definition of politics to very narrow partisan politics, there is less in human concerns that are political.

Chuck leaving the post office with his mail and friends, Slug and Creepo. Manley Hot Springs, November 1981.

But in terms of group action that affects all of us, there is little that isn't political.

For instance, the Catholic Church elects the Pope. Conservatives and liberals throw their weight for one candidate or another. If God is working there, he's working through a political system. Same with the Episcopal Church.

For the past several Episcopal Conventions there has been a stiff fight over allowing women to be priests. This would appear to be a spiritual or religious question, but it's settled politically. There was no commandment from God. It was a group of men and women who voted.

As I look around me, I see the school as somewhat political, the Post Office and the Highway Department as somewhat political. Recently, the school district, that is some administrators of the school district, were pushing for the formation of a third-class borough. Ostensibly it would gather more revenue through property taxes of the Pipeline to benefit the school. A political process and a political·decision.

Not too long ago the Fairbanks North Star Borough School District was heavily slanted towards Baptist teachers because the superintendent of schools was a Baptist. He hired a lot of Baptist teachers so the whole school system slanted towards Baptist teaching. The superintendent has pretty broad powers and the board can go along or oppose his actions, but he has a lot of authority.

There are many reasons for people not being involved in politics, not being politically aware. One of them is sheer laziness, and certainly I fall into this category too. It takes effort to maintain political awareness and concern yourself

L-R: Diane Dart and Liza Vernet painting a presidential campaign sign in the Dart home, August 1972.

Chuck Dart, Representative Pappy Moss and Joe Cooper at the Manley Hot Springs school dedication 1980.

with issues. What most of us would like to do is have a father in politics, turn over our political destiny to a man that we have complete trust in and not bother us. Very few people concern themselves with the functioning of government. When you consider that nearly a third of our wages go to taxes, we should be heavily interested. And we need to follow through.

Often we'll vote for a person who has expressed a philosophy we like, but it is rare to let our wishes be known to him once he is in office. It is even rarer if we do request him to take a certain stand or vote a certain way, to write a word of praise if he does it. Most politicians, even those I don't like, are poorly treated by the public. Their actions are not appreciated.

True, some men will use their positions to feather their own nests, but that is not as common now as it was a hundred years ago. Even Nixon, Agnew, Bobby Baker, and Tyung Sun Park I believe, maybe I want to believe, are more the exception than the rule. I think that most men go into politics motivated by principle rather than by avarice. They may also be motivated by ego and wanting the adulation of the crowd, but I believe most of them are basically honest.

As far as women and politics go, there is still a sizable segment of the population that feel the woman should be in the home. Dixie Dayo was an active worker for Mike Dalton one summer and she ran into it repeatedly right here in Manley Hot Springs. People made no bones about it saying, "A woman just shouldn't be in politics." There is also a segment of the population that feels this is true about Natives or Blacks. It's a prejudice that they have and they're not going to shake it easily.

I think there has been a leap forward in the status of women and I look to see continuing improvement in women's positions. Here again, there will be diehards that will go to their graves opposing women's equality and women's rights, but I think these people are on the decline rather than on the increase. I have a strong feeling we are becoming more enlightened.

All of us males have been made aware that we have unjustly treated women in various aspects of their lives. You'd have to be pretty cement-headed not to be aware of this and to recognize it. That doesn't mean we don't retain some of our poor habits and thought patterns, but I think there is a general trend toward enlightenment in most aspects of women's situation.

For some men it is a threat to their sense of masculinity to do what is traditionally a female function such as cooking or cleaning the house or taking care of the kids. Once in a while someone walks in and sees me doing dishes and makes a comment about it, but what the hell? Somebody's got to do the dishes. I don't feel any stigma attached to any form of labor that has honor and dignity to it. Anything that's constructive and productive, whether it's done by male or female has honor and dignity.

Those things destructive to self or others don't have honor. I feel strongly about some areas. Specifically, I could never be a drug pusher. I'm thinking about alcohol and tobacco as well as so-called hard drugs. I would much rather be looked down upon for doing dishes or cooking than selling cigarettes or booze to people who shouldn't have them.

Generally in our house we have broken from the traditional stereotyped roles. Gladys does a lot of things that would be considered by some people as being masculine spheres of labor. She will eagerly work planting potatoes or farming. Of course, she grew up in a farm situation. Many farm wives shared the male occupations of the farm, but the husbands did not share the female occupations. Actually in many farm households, the wife worked alongside the husband in the fields and when they finished, she prepared supper and did dishes while he rested. In many instances throughout the world, particularly nonindustrialized countries, women have taken a disproportionate share of the burden of work.

Chuck Dart at a Japanese inn, Kamakura, Japan. January 1977.

Chapter Three: The Crash

The Crash

Gladys asked Chuck to tell the following story — a significant event in the Dart family.

It was on a Saturday evening after work in late June of 1952. We had had supper and I was sitting on the floor reading the paper. We were living on Wolff Run, which is near the end of Phillips Field runway in Fairbanks. We lived there for a while and with lots of airplanes coming and going, we never paid attention to them. But I became aware of this one when I heard a sudden change in engine sound.

Very soon I heard a crash. I ran outside and could see nothing until the airplane burst into flames. It was about two hundred feet away in some brush and very close to some tall spruce trees. I ran over there and I could see that the airplane was upside down at the base of some large white spruce. As I got about twenty-five feet away from the airplane all I could see in the cockpit was a sack of potatoes that had broken open.

Suddenly fire engulfed my legs like a flame thrower. Well, my father had burned to death when he was starting a fire with what was sold to him as kerosene but was in fact a mixture of kerosene and gasoline. The thought that went through my head was, I'm going to die like Dad. I presume some kind of gasline had ruptured in the airplane which caused this stream of flaming gasoline. But there wasn't enough gasoline to sustain the fire. It was just a flash and then it was gone. There was an eighteen year old boy named John Workman that was camping on our ground with his family. I realized he was behind me when he yelled, "Look out Chuck!"

The pilot was aware there were people nearby and yelled, "I'm over here!" from inside the airplane. We went around to the other side of the airplane and could see he was still strapped in his seat upside down with his head hanging down. Another sack of potatoes had taken out a small triangular window when the crash occurred. The pilot got his arms and head through that opening and we reached in and grabbed him under the armpits. We really pulled hard and I'm sure he was pushing with his feet too. The broken bits of glass in the window frame which I had tried to remove with no luck began to bite into his back. There was no choice but to pull him on through.

We got him out of there and about ten or fifteen feet away from the plane he wanted to sit down and rest. We didn't want him to. As it turned out we just got him out of there when the fire really took off and the spruce trees went swoosh like they do when they get hot enough to go up in a fast fire.

The pilot turned out to be Cliff Fairchild. He was hauling freight to Fort Yukon when the plane went down. He was pretty lucky to get out with a few small cuts and rather minor burns on the backs of his ankles. I never did talk to Fairchild about the incident but his wife came by that evening and thanked us profusely.

The *News-Miner* and *Jessen's Weekly* ran articles about the accident. It was kind of embarrassing to be thought of as a hero. People would tell me how proud I should be. To me it wasn't that big a thing. It wasn't heroic in terms of planning something where you were deliberately risking your neck or extending your limits. It was just something that happened. I wouldn't have chosen to do it. It was just the position I was thrust into. I did have a recurring nightmare for some time after that about an airplane across a valley that would crash and burn. I was never able to get there. In the dream it was obvious from the start that I would never be able to make it all the way across to do any good. I'm thankful that no one was badly injured in the actual situation I was faced with.

Chapter Four: Gladys Reed In Minnesota

Automba

I was born August 12, 1924 in Moose Lake, Minnesota, but our family lived in a little village called Automba about sixty miles from where Chuck grew up. In the local Chippewa language it means "sweet little village." Logging and lumber were the industries that formed Automba but they disappeared six years before I was born. The forest fire of 1918 burned about sixty square miles of Minnesota and completely wiped out logging. By the time

Threshing grain near Grafton, N.D. 1911.

Minnesota Historical Society

1924 rolled around Automba was a farming town and the population was quickly declining.

At first my father owned a farm, then he sold the farm and moved into town becoming the only businessman. He built a hotel, sold it, and built a general store that included the post office. He was the train depot custodian, kept three cows and gave haircuts. On top of that he traveled widely as an evangelical Lutheran minister and raised twelve kids.

My mother had thirteen children. One died in infancy, but the rest reached adulthood. Ten of us are still living. I was the seventh. It was a common saying that my mother had twelve children but she raised twenty-five. We were always having guests stay with us from the Finnish Apostolic Lutheran Church.

Gladys' father's family in Finland circa 1945. L-R sitting: John's second wife's adopted son, John's second wife, John Aijala Riitijoki (Matthew's father), Alma (Matthew's sister). Back standing: Alma's son, Alma's daughter Sylvia, Harry, Sylvia's husband Gunnar Lehti.

At 17 my father and a friend of his the same age immigrated to the United States from Finland. It was a case of restless youth looking for work in a world where jobs were not to be found. Naturally he looked to America and soon settled in the Finnish community in Minnesota. He was a man of many interests and, of course, his life reflected that. There were many opportunities to move to other towns but his heart was in Automba. In fact about fifteen years ago my mother and father were the only residents. Population of two. Now my niece has moved back with her family so the town is growing again. It is now five.

In Finnish my father's name was Matti Rittijoki, which means Reed River, the place he grew up. Traditionally in Finland you are named after the place you live. If you bought property you took the name of the previous owner. So if someone bought the hot springs they would take the last name of Dart. That system worked all right in Finland when people didn't move too often, but it would be disastrous in the United States now with our high transiency.

In order to simplify things for people who couldn't understand Finnish, my father changed his name from Riitiyoki to Reed. My mother's maiden name in Finnish is Jarvenpaa, which means "river's head" or "source". Her family Anglicized it to Jarvis.

In 1909, when my father came to America, he spoke only Finnish. It was a tremendous problem for him. Along with that he found quite a bit of prejudice against Finns where he was working in northern Minnesota. He was often ridiculed and at one point he was about to be beaten up. A big, muscular man, a Minnesota Indian, came to his rescue. They became lifelong friends after that.

Our home was definitely bilingual. Since Father was trying to learn English, the rule was that we talked to him in English and he talked to us in

Gladys' parents, Edna Sophia and Matt Reed's golden wedding anniversary 1965.

Chuck and Gladys Dart Collection

Grandma Reed taking a break from baking at the Dart home in Manley Hot Springs. The chairs are draped with her fine hand-woven rag-rugs. Summer, 1982.

English. My mother spoke both languages very well.

I learned Finn all right, but especially this last thirty years in Alaska, I haven't had much chance to practice. Surprisingly, when we made a trip back to Finland this summer, I was able to communicate with relatives who could only speak Finn. The influence of those early years was profound enough to carry it through.

I feel lucky to have grown up with two languages and I'm richer for it. The only time more than one language confuse children is when a totally new language is forced upon them and they are required to discard their first one. That is what happened in many Alaskan villages with the Native languages.

Along with the Finnish language we had a strong Finnish national spirit in our home. We kept up on news of Finland whenever we could. As far as other customs go, we were limited in my household by the fact that my father and mother converted to the Lutheran Church and it contained many inhibitions about dancing, card playing, and any type of liquor. But in essence I would say it was a bicultural home. When people ask about my background, I always say Finnish.

Yet my father was definitely American. His loyalties were here. Shortly after my parents were married they had a chance to go back to Finland and receive a large inheritance. But their choice was easy. He had found his place and his opportunity here.

Sauna

Our home was a very stable one. All of us kids were raised in the same house and it is still in the family now. Actually the house was originally built as a school. My father bought it after a new brick schoolhouse was built. He remodeled it himself. In Finland vocational education is an important part of high school so by the time my father finished he was an accomplished cabinet maker and carpenter.

Probably my favorite part of the house was a 10' x 14' log cabin sauna bathhouse on the back corner of the lot. We heated it regularly once a week or more often if needed. The sauna is very important to Finns. It is the preferred place to give birth and my father was born in the sauna at his parent's house.

The stove was made from a fifty-five gallon drum with a flat piece of metal put on top to hold rocks. We had two metal containers to hold water right next to the stove and three platforms at different levels to sit on. Usually you started at a lower level and quickly went to the highest one to get the full impact of the steam. We made the steam by throwing water on the hot rocks. It is also a Finnish custom to tie young tender birch branches in a bundle and pat yourself with them to quicken the sweating. We stayed inside until we built up a good sweat, then cooled off in the dressing room. Three times in the sauna was usually enough, then we'd wash off with soap and water. After that most Finns go out and roll in the snow or jump into a cold lake. We used to do that for fun, but as a regular bath we just rinsed off with progressively cooler water.

You would think that it would be a very exhausting experience. If you regulate the heat right and recognize your own tolerances, it is just the opposite. I remember putting a hard day's work in on a farm, planting potatoes or bringing in the hay, then taking a sauna and feeling like dancing all night. But you have to build up to that.

The first time I took Chuck to a Finnish bath in Fairbanks, I got a little excited and overdid it. I threw water on the rocks too fast, forced the steam, so he had to just get up and leave the room. He became quite angry with me. He said, "You crazy Finns! Even the Russians had enough sense to keep their heads outside the tents."

It has to do with your general health too. Sometimes Chuck tolerates a much hotter bath than I do. If you've had surgery or been very sick, you really have to watch it.

41

We Liked to be Outside

Summer and winter we liked to be outside. Sure there were a few quiet games and reading, but we were all involved in sports. The boys were very good at it, and since we lived in a small town frequently the girls had to fill in when there weren't enough players. We were on football teams and I played baseball from when I was very small. I got good enough at baseball to be the pitcher for several years on the school team. We also had normal track meet events and long distance running. We started from the steps of my father's store and went for a mile. There would be many adults that came just to watch.

Summertime we'd all pile in the back of a truck and go swimming. Wintertime it was skating and sledding, but not skiing for some reason. Mostly we skated on creeks and rivers. I remember my brother spending hours of time every winter making a skating path around our property. He iced down the path with buckets of water in all kinds of intricate designs. He became an excellent skater.

Another place to play, unique to our town was the abandoned lumber sheds. After the fire in 1918, the buildings stayed empty and gradually started to fall apart. They became giant playhouses for us. We would play tag running along narrow planks and jumping from platform to platform. When you got to the highest place you were twenty-five to thirty feet off the ground. It's just amazing that in all the years we played in there we didn't have one major accident. Every once in a while someone would fall from the ceiling to the floor and not be hurt.

One day I was running along a narrow platform, hanging on like a monkey to the studs as I went and all of a sudden both hands let go. I had the brief instant of falling the tremendous distance from the roof to the ground. I still panic now when I'm at a height.

Everyone had gardens and the largest were for potatoes. In the spring, we went from farm to farm helping plant and in the fall helping to dig them up. In fact, they used to have a week long vacation from school called "Potato Digging Week" so all the kids could help.

I was pretty much of a tomboy. I liked outside things and I detested housework. Luckily, I had two older sisters and I could push off sweeping or doing dishes on them because they were so much better at it than I was. To this day, I feel guilty about it although I certainly did enough chores. There were cows to be milked, gardens, canning, and berry picking. Along with the things we grew and goods from my father's store, we had venison for our winter meat. My father was an excellent deer hunter.

Our Store

Before the 1918 fire, Automba had quite a few businesses. It was a thriving community. Six lumber mills went twenty-four hours a day and we had hotels and a bank. But from the time I remember, my father's store was the only one in town.

Actually the one I remember was his third. The first two were destroyed by fire. I remember being in the first grade in 1930, looking out the window of school and seeing the store building burn to the ground. Besides general merchandise to supply a country farming community, he had a gas station, feed store, post office, and barbershop. For refrigeration he dragged in blocks of ice in the wintertime and kept them under

Minnesota Historical Society.

Princeton potato planters. Minnesota circa 1920.

sawdust in a back shed all summer.

Each time after the store burned down, my father was in business the next day out of an empty house in town. Then he rebuilt and restocked from the excellent credit he had established. The last store is still there. My mother sold it to the township as a town hall. They call it the "Little White House."

School

We had a one-room school, but it was in a beautiful two-story brick building. There weren't enough students for separate grades so I went to all eight grades in that one room. The year I graduated they consolidated the school with one seven miles away and closed up.

One of the influences in my elementary school years was the fact there were so few children. We had to learn how to get along in a more integrated system than in most public schools nowadays. We didn't have the segregation by sex or age that larger schools have. I think it was a good thing to have the influence of the older kids and as we grew older, we also had to be responsible for the younger children.

I had only three classmates in the first grade but I can remember being engaged in activities very comfortably with eighth grade boys and girls. Being in a one-room school I was exposed to much of the teaching at the advanced grades even though I wasn't an active participant in those grades. Because of those advantages, I was accelerated a grade in school. That meant I graduated from the eighth grade when I was twelve.

Lack of numbers also changed the kind of games we played. If we wanted to have a good time we had to include everybody with different amounts of skill, coordination and size.

We had regular standard academic subjects, but no formal P. E. classes. And anything we got in the way of music was only because we had a teacher who was interested. We did have one teacher who played the piano well and we liked to sing at home, but that's the extent of any musical development. I still feel musically illiterate. Overall though it was a good experience being a student in a one-room school because teaching in a one-room school has been most of my professional life.

High school was twenty-five miles away. We got there by school bus and other than getting caught in a couple blizzards, it was just a long ride. High school had quite a few more students and teachers and different classes. My favorite classes were in language arts. I used to spend time creating stories although I never wrote them down. Mostly I remember writing poetry. When we had class assignments in poetry, there was a lot of cheating because I wrote it for a lot of other students too.

Leaving Home

There were no jobs in Automba. In most families, with the exception of an oldest son staying home to take over a farm, everyone left. My older brothers and sisters had gone to the East Coast where we had relatives and had gotten jobs in factories. When I got out of high school at sixteen, that was the thing for me to do too — go to the city and find a job. There was also this general feeling among young people to just go, you know. Go to the biggest city in the world and experience it. And then by the time I got out of high school in '41, the war was on and the boys were being drafted.

I stayed home for a part of the first year out of

Gladys' high school graduation photograph, 1941.

school to help run the family store and I was there when Pearl Harbor was bombed in December. Soon after that, in January, I left to go to Massachusetts to find a job. First I worked as a clerk in a laundry. When the cleaning job was not a good one, I heard about it. I hated having to listen to people say unkind things about the business I had no control over. I quit as soon as I had a chance at another job. I finished that year working in a fraternity house helping with the cooking and cleaning.

Meanwhile my father hadn't been able to travel much because he was taking care of business in Automba. He wrote and asked me to come home for three months to fill in for him. I did and then kept going west. A year in the East Coast cities was enough.

My aunt and uncle Grace and Bill Jarvis lived in Renton, Washington so I went to see them and got a job in the war plant for Boeing as a riveter on the B-17 and B-29 bombers. I enjoyed the work even though we were doing a job that wasn't usually women's work. Every other woman was doing it as well, including older women. There were women welders and riveters and mechanics. We

Front row: Eino Alaspa with tie, Jackie Alaspa, Lenny and Gary Jarvis. Second row: Bobby Alaspa held by Lillian Alaspa, Grace Jarvis, Matt Reed, Esther Jarvis, Eleanor Alaspa, Lorraine Martin. Back row: Violet Martin, Bill Jarvis, Gladys Dart and her sister Emily Alaspa. Renton, Washington circa 1942.

Duplex roommates and neighbors in Renton, Washington 1943. L-R: Gladys, Betty Corcorin, Gladys' sister Emily and Violet Martin. Gladys and Emily owned the Willis automobile.

were exposed to women doing jobs equal to men more than at any other time. It was just the period that caused it. We were at war and women were needed.

In the Army Now

I worked in the plant for two years when we received word that my brother had been killed in France. I decided what I really wanted to do was serve in the Medical Corps of the Armed Forces. Another girl who worked in the factory and I went down to the Marine office. It wasn't open. We went to the Navy office, the Waves, but they weren't open either. Finally we went to the Army recruiting office and they were open so that's how I got into the Army.

The recruiter told me that if I enlisted I had my choice of type of work and locality. I told them I wanted to be in the Medical Corps anywhere west of the Mississippi. As it turned out, I took my basic in Ohio and never got west of the Mississippi. I did get medical training, but hardly had a chance to work in the Medical Corps.

After the initial training, I was sent to Miami Beach to stay in one of those $100 a day hotels the Army kept. My first assignment was working in a lab. I became very interested in that and then after a week a doctor doing research with animals invited me to move into his section. After seeing the work for a few days, I became entranced. In a couple weeks when I had become totally immersed and excited about the whole thing, they pulled me out to do office

L-R: Pvt. Poole, Pvt. Ramaker, Pvt. Raymond and Pvt. Gladys Reed, 1945.

work. I rebelled to the Colonel as much as I dared, saying that east of the Mississippi and office work were the last things I wanted when I had enlisted. Why did he have to transfer me?

He just spread my aptitude test scores out in a big fan and said the tests show I could do anything, and I would probably be happy in the office once I settled down. He was right.

The office was across from the beach. I could look out the window and see sand and ocean. The job was to straighten out payroll problems of the soldiers sent there for rehabilitation. Some of them had been prisoners-of-war, some were wounded, and all of them had payrolls messed up in one way or another.

We had a lot of freedom to race around in a jeep to the different hotels the men stayed in because some of them couldn't move. It got to be a neat thing because we weren't doing the same thing every day. The officer assigned to us was lax and easy to get along with. I got into a routine of bringing my bathing suit and going on the beach during lunch hours.

From Miami I was sent to Long Island to another office job. By then the war was over and we couldn't wait to get out. While the war was going on I felt I was making a contribution, but after it was over, I lost interest. I wasn't much of a soldier anyway. They used to say, "She does a wonderful job, but she's a bit too unconventional." I was always being caught for not being in proper dress. I had to wash windows because I wasn't wearing a neck tie. Or wash windows because my hair was over my collar. Or peel potatoes because I said something I wasn't supposed to say. It was always something so I never made more than corporal.

When I look back on it now I'm glad I was in the Army and I'm glad it's over. I feel very loyal to our country, but I'd question blind patriotism. I'm sympathetic with the people who refused to go into the Army during the Vietnam War. You really have to think through the reasons why. Another thing I feel strongly about is the comment "giving your son for your country." You can't give anybody's life away. If they go into the service and are killed, they are giving up their life. A parent isn't making any kind of gift in that sense.

Chapter Five: Gladys in Education

Choosing a Career

When I got out of the Army, that was the point of major decision. I had reached that age where I would have to decide where I was going next. I knew that if I didn't do it now, I probably wouldn't do it.

When I started checking into colleges and universities, I also thought in terms of traveling. I made my big plan. I got all of the literature and enrolled in the University of Alaska for the first year. The next year I wanted to go to the University of Hawaii, the third year to the University of New Zealand, and the fourth year to the University of Mexico, and then I was going to decide where I was going to go from there. I got all the catalogs and plans. I came to the University of Alaska in Fairbanks in September of '47, and I'm still in Alaska.

The G. I. Bill was going to carry me through for about half of my education. I knew that working for the other half and to become a doctor was probably more than I could handle so I gave up medicine and thought of business administration.

When my Uncle Eino Alaspa heard, he said I would never be happy doing that. I said, "Well, what's wrong with making a lot of money?"

"You'd just never be happy, I know you won't," he said. So we did a lot of talking and I did a lot of thinking and decided he was right. I decided on education, but had secondary education on my mind when I started out. After I married and had small children, I switched over to elementary.

I also visited with my father's sister on the East Coast after I got out of the service. She tried to talk me into going into business with her. "Let's start a restaurant first," she said. I told her I had no interest or money to do it. She said, "I have the money and I know we can make a success of it."

I asked her how it was with her life; she wasn't that well educated and still she was independent. She said, "Well, the only reason why I am what I am today is that I couldn't stand to have a husband who could work harder than I could." She was motivated by that source. She had become a very wealthy woman just by her own industry. I guess I had never thought about how some women had to make choices in their life to have a career or family. I never thought about the influence a man might have on a woman's life.

I've thought about her every now and then. She influenced me to believe that a woman can do what she wants to if she really wants to do it. But then, I can easily say that because the men who have an influence on my life would have given me the right to do that. I've never been in a position when I didn't have that right.

I've never felt discrimination against me as a woman. I can see it in the world around me, but the things that I have wanted have come to me. If I would have wanted to have a career in education administration I would probably have been blocked simply because I was a woman. That's the way it used to be. But then I never tried because business administration in education is not my thing. Classroom teaching is where I feel I belong, where I am most effective.

University of Alaska

It was really a neat time to go to the University. The enrollment was so small, and Fairbanks was so small, we really had the feeling that we were part of a pioneer culture. Everybody seemed to know everybody on a first-name speaking basis, from the University President to the girl who lived in the next room.

It was also a very fortunate time to go to school because the average student age level was older and they were more mature. We had a challenging type of intellect among the students in the classroom. That was because most of the students were ex-G.I.'s. They were going to school under the G. I. Bill of Rights.

Most of the people were from outside of Alaska. In fact, the first full-blooded Eskimo graduated from the University in 1950. Arthur Nagozrak from Nome. He was a classmate of ours. There were other Alaskan Natives there, but they were in the minority. The larger percentage was from Outside.

Chuck and Gladys at Farmers Loop, Fairbanks 1948.

I can remember one of the professors telling us he was going to be glad when the G. I. Bill ran out and he could teach high school students again. That would be easier because we wouldn't just accept answers just because they came from the authority in front of the classroom. Sometimes it felt that we weren't getting the answers that we thought we should. For instance, if we had themes that were rated less than we thought they deserved, we felt that we had the right to know why and would question it. We weren't always ready to accept what they gave us. And for another thing, to come out of the Army and then be plopped into a dorm where we were regulated by hours that say you must be in by ten o'clock was to say the least, aggravating.

The University looked so incredibly different then. There were all plain gray buildings and very bare. The library was the second floor of the museum and the old museum was the gym. They looked like gray mental institutions. You need to look at pictures to believe it.

When I first arrived the total enrollment was a couple of hundred. One of the semesters I was up there it dropped to less than a

Chuck, circa 1946.

hundred. But it had its advantages. Students were much more intimate with the whole structure. To me that was an advantage, probably from my background of living in a small community situation. That's one of the reasons I came up here. I think it was also a disadvantage because of our limited number of faculty.

I met Chuck at the University of Alaska the first year, and that's why I still happen to be here in Alaska and didn't go to the University of Hawaii my second year. It was strange because he was born and raised sixty miles from where I was born and raised, and our high schools were rivals. Still we didn't meet until we came to the University of Alaska. The outstanding immediate appeal was Chuck as an articulate intellect, that probably impressed me more than anything. You know he's good looking, but not that good looking. I would say his articulateness and he's an intellect for sure.

Matt Reed, Diane Dart and Edna Reed at Chico, California 1952.

Soon all the other places had faded, Hawaii, New Zealand, Mexico. I could see that my future was in Alaska. I knew that my future also was in education. I worked full-time plus going to school. It was with the Alaska Communications System in Fairbanks, the telegraph office. Because of the type of work I got to know many people in Fairbanks and really got to like it in the 40's. It was still a small-town atmosphere, very friendly. It was a kind of open-door hospitality.

In 1950, Chuck and I were married and immediately began raising our family. We continued with school and decided to leave Alaska to complete our Bachelor degrees. We left for the school year because of the small education department at the University. There was only one professor on the staff there and we didn't feel like we were being adequately trained for the profession. Finally we decided on Chico State in California and went there for three years.

Jim Dart circa 1960.

John Dart at the Henderson Mine in the Ester area, 1954.

Raising a Family in School

When I graduated at Chico in January of '54, we had Diane and Johnny and I was expecting Jimmy. So Johnny was born in Chico our second year there, and we were back in Alaska when Jim was born in Fairbanks, August of '54.

Actually, academically I did my best when I had the most responsibilities at home and a heavy schedule at school. My only straight-A year in college was when I did my practice teaching, took night classes, had the two small children at home, was expecting the

"Our first trip Outside with Diane on our way to school at Chico State, August 1951."

53

third, and also had two nephews staying with us. But necessity demanded organization. If I had been single and attending college, much of that time would have been spent in social activities and a more lax schedule.

Chuck and I shared a lot. There always has been a sharing. There hasn't been any labor divided by the role of a man and woman in our household. Chuck is a better cook than I am, for example. And he's very good with child raising. We worked very well without planning any kind of division. The only time I remember any discussion about "you do this" type of thing was after John was born. There are eighteen months difference between Diane and John and we were both going to school. We made the arrangement where if Diane woke up during the night, Chuck would wake and take care of her. And if Johnny woke up I would take care of him, of course, because I was nursing him. It was a one-bedroom apartment with all four of us in that room. Diane would cry at night and I would not hear her, and Johnny would cry at night and Chuck wouldn't hear him. It worked out very well.

I suppose in the '50's that was an uncommon arrangement because I always considered myself very lucky in this aspect. I also think that I have given him the same freedom. So although there's an awareness of the roles we play and that we mix in a way that other families don't, I don't think of it as any big thing. It's just a very natural arrangement in our home. When I think of my good luck in this arrangement I think, how nice that Chuck enjoys cooking when I hate it so much. He didn't marry me for my housekeeping talents, that's for sure. And when I'm teaching, Chuck does almost one hundred percent of the cooking. During the summer, I work in the greenhouses and there is a shared labor there.

A Career in Education

As soon as I graduated from college, there was only one thing that I wanted to do — teach. While still at Chico both of us had an offer to teach in Cordova. That's when I found out I was expecting Jimmy sometime in August. It just wasn't practical for us to accept that Cordova position so we returned to Fairbanks.

Early in '55, while Jim was just a baby and the other two children were very small too, I was told about an opening in Illiamna. I wanted that job so badly. I was ready to pack up my family and take them all there. Chuck didn't want me to accept the job because it was an unfamiliar town and he didn't know what there would be for him. He didn't want the full economic responsibility for the famiy to rest on my teaching job. He talked me out of that one, but that's the only time he ever did. I don't think I would have ever let him talk me out of another one — even if he would have tried. He never did.

Chuck realized from the outset how important my career in education was to me. He has also made the comment that if I would have wanted to work just to have a job he would have tried to influence me not to work away from home, especially in the early years of our marriage. However, because there were teaching opportunities open to me he cooperated in every way and supported me one hundred percent in pursuing a career in education.

The fall of '55 I accepted a position teaching in

Diane's Episcopal confirmation in Bertie Mason's cabin. L-R front: Mary Clements, Gladys, Judy Woods, Bertie Mason, Bishop Gordon's wife holding flowers. Back: Diane Dart, Sally Woods, Circa 1962.

Jim and John Dart in a helicopter. Tanana 1961.

the Fairbanks school system. It was in the College area. There wasn't a school there. I taught first grade in the basement of the Presbyterian Church at the foot of the hill.

As it turned out, fate worked it's magic anyway. If we would have gone to Illiamna we would not have heard about Hot Springs. Because we stayed in Fairbanks we found out about the sale of the hot springs. I'm sure Chuck will tell you that story. Anyway, we had an opportunity that comes to few in a lifetime and purchased the hot springs, which is just an incredible property in an Arctic land.

Chuck spent that winter at Hot Springs building the first greenhouse and getting ready for the season. I had the children in Fairbanks and hired a girl to stay with me and take care of the children during the day while I taught next door in the church. It worked out very well. The day after school was out in the spring of '56, I came out to Hot Springs with the children to join Chuck.

Jim Dart's 4th birthday, August 31, 1958. L-R front: Barbara Strandberg, Chuck Dart, David Monroe, Steve Strandberg, Holmberg girl sitting on Gladys' lap. Row two: Clara Holmberg, Hazel Dayo holding Dixie Dayo, Becky, Shirley, Rodney and Ralph Holmberg, Johnathan Blackburn, Jim Dart, John Dart. Back row: Carol Lee Blackburn, Diane Dart, Dawn Monroe, Jeanie Blackburn, Robert "Bolo" Thompson.

End-of-the-school-year party at the old cabin school with the bathhouse in the background, circa 1960. L-R: Lena Woods, unidentified swinging at pinata, Billy Lanning, Sally Woods, Mary Lanning, Freddie Burk.

Hot Springs School

When we moved here there was no school and very few children. The N. C. Store's manager and wife had an adopted daughter who took correspondence school and there was one family that had preschool age children. I taught our daughter on correspondence her first year. Any parent could teach correspondence if one of them had the equivalency of a high school degree.

In the fall of '58, there were ten school children and we were put on what they called "special school status." The community had to provide a building, a certified teacher and ten school-age children in order to establish a special school. The Territorial Department of Education approved the 16' x 20' log cabin on our property next to the bath as the school and approved of myself as the certified teacher.

Chuck's arrangement was that he would supply the building, the heat, which was hot springs water, light and janitorial services for $100 a month. The light in those days was the Coleman lanterns. Chuck bought the light plant and increased the contract price to $150 a month. That's quite a comparison to a school today.

School was to begin in September, but we had absolutely no supplies. Chuck fixed up the building. He cut the legs off two tables so they'd be short enough for the children to sit at with their Blazo box chairs. Then he took a 4' x 8' plyboard and painted it with black slate paint. That was our blackboard. We collected all the pencils and paper in town that we could and used books we had around at home.

The first two months I taught using any ingenuity on hand to keep the children going. It was quite a challenge for the first year out in the village and my second year of teaching. I got so frustrated by the lack of supplies and books, but it also taught me a lesson well. There was quite a lot of creative-type material if you made the most out of what you have. I pretty much used local inspiration like descriptions of the area for themes to teach children writing. Finally, on Halloween, supplies and teaching materials arrived.

I taught in that 16' x 20' log cabin until 1960-61. When I had nineteen students in 1960, that was a bit crowded. I had to plan the Christmas program that year so once the children were on stage they wouldn't move for the remainder of the program. There wasn't much room for activity with nineteen students performing and most of the community there to watch. That's when the State decided we needed a little bit more room.

Chuck built the building that is our present house, 52' x 26' with plastic walls full length from floor to ceiling along the southside 52' wall and half of each end. We put a partition in the center and used half of the building as the school which became 26' x 26'. Then during the summer we packed all of the school supplies and put them into storage for the summer and use the whole building as our home. Each fall we would rent the space for

Manley Hot Springs school, September 1970. Back row, L-R: Mike Fleagle, Julie Frick, Kenny Thumma, Pat Thumma, Frank Fleagle. Front row: Jay DeLima, Jerry Beth Fleagle, Teresa DeLima, Tim Fleagle.

the school year and unpack the stuff and put up the partition again. It was very convenient for me, but Chuck would have to accomodate his activities so it wouldn't distract the students. As a matter of fact, he discouraged any activity in the home other than quiet social visiting.

In the fall of '63, the school downtown was built. We moved to Fairbanks at that time so Diane could go to high school. Since we weren't going to be here in Manley, a more permanent school building was needed.

The One-Room School

The one-room school is where my heart is. That's where it's always been. I'm one of those fortunate people that had an opportunity to pursue their career in exactly the setting that they wanted. If I had my choice of anything, it would still be in a one-room school and, of course, in Hot Springs. I just have a feeling that I can perform my best in that kind of a situation. It's the greatest challenge for me and I see rewards in teaching in a one-room school that can't be duplicated elsewhere. If I am to be remembered for anything, I would hope it's for my daily performance in the classroom.

1983 Hot Springs school Christmas program. L-R: Glenn Evans, Derek Joiner, Sean Carney, Gladys Dart, Patrick Hook, Mark Evans and Laura Hollingsworth looking at Santa Claus.

The main thing that I've noticed in the years that I've taught in a one-room school is that you have a built-in system of review and preview I call it. It's an ideal. You have a built-in system for remedial-type teaching and also for gifted, or enrichment teaching. It's done everyday in an ordinary classroom situation.

If you have a child who missed something — some concept along the way in math, in spelling, in any subject area — while you are teaching that concept at a lower lever, they can easily be a part of that learning process. It's done in a very unobtrusive way. All the child needs to do is just pay attention while the concept is being taught. Nobody but you or he need know it and sometimes not even you the teacher. Children have a way of perking their attention at times like this and they do it naturally. They are aware of their needs.

The same is true of enrichment. For example, a child at the primary grade level might suddenly become interested in what is going on at the upper grade level. He simply quits what he's doing and pays attention. Sometimes you can become involved in an activity and the whole classroom will suddenly stop whatever they're doing and congregate in a circle around that activity. Because it is such a closeknit type situation, children can do this without being embarrassed. A sixth or seventh grade student can participate in an activity with primary children. It's a joy to watch that type of built-in motivation system.

I really stress independent work habits. I start them right there at the first grade level. In the one-room school situation you have to concentrate on a one-to-one level with the children who are coming to school for the first time at the beginning primary ages. If you have a whole room full of upper primary and intermediate children who cannot sit down and do their work you couldn't possibly give that time. That doesn't mean that they don't need to come to you. They do constantly, but it has to be done with certain organization.

I've had run-ins with other educators about the philosophy that you have to have ultimate patience in the classroom. To me, it's necessary for the children to know that we have emotions too, that we can have good days as well as bad days. If a child displeases me, I want him to know that he's displeasing me. On the other hand, if a child pleases me, it's just as necessary for me to tell him that. It doesn't bother me for a child to know that I'm very angry about something that he did. And I can love him. I can cry with him and laugh with him depending upon the situation. I encourage them to do the same with me.

I am a strict disciplinarian. I establish the fact right from the beginning and also maintain a reputation for it. The first job that you are there for as a teacher is to create an atmosphere where children can learn. You are not going to do

Manley Hot Springs students 1981. L-R: Alex Neff, Erin McDougal, Kelly Jacobs, Daryl Methvin, Mrs. Damaris Richmond-Mortvedt and Amy Evans in the sled, Heather Redington, Tonya Schlentner, Joee Ray Redington, Mark Evans, Glenn Evans.

it in a disruptive environment. It's easier to establish on that strict level. Then from there on you proceed with a philosophy that they get as much freedom as they can handle.

In Spring 1977, I retired with hot springs projects in mind. When plans for developing the hot springs were abandoned and I found myself without a satisfactory creative outlet, I looked back to teaching. Of course, by then Damaris Richmond-Mortvedt was the Manley Hot Springs school teacher so I looked elsewhere for a position. When I made my mind up that I was ready to go back to teaching I called up Colin Baxter and found myself teaching in Ruby the fall of '78.

Ruby was certainly as beautiful as I had heard. It was a bit different situation from what it was in Hot Springs. In Ruby I was one of four teachers in a school kindergarten to high school. I handled the entire program for sixth through eighth with the exception of P. E. And although I'm thankful for my time at Ruby I found I really missed Hot Springs more than I had anticipated. When I first left Hot Springs, I thought, Ruby isn't that far away that I can't visit Manley often during the year. But Christmas was the only time I got back there actually. Transportation was quite a problem. The only reason I even got out Christmastime was the fact that I was helicoptered out with Santa Claus. So after a year away from home there is no doubt that I want to spend my life in Hot Springs.

Altona Brown and Gladys Dart looking at Altona's old photos in Ruby. Gladys was interviewing Altona to expand the Ruby school local history materials, March 1979.

Chapter Six: Chuck and Gladys Dart in
Hot Springs

Opportunity of a Lifetime

Gladys:

We made our first trip to Hot Springs in 1950, over the Fourth of July weekend. A person only needs to make a short trip to Hot Springs to know if that property is available he's going to take it. It's an opportunity that comes to few in a lifetime. At that time there was no reason for us to believe that the property would be available to us in five years. I can remember walking in that area and saying, "If you had a dream come true, it would be to have a place like this someday." Suddenly five years later, it was ours.

I can honestly say the same thing today and even more so after being here for twenty-three years. I often think, "How could we be so lucky?" This land is very special to me. It's just an indescribable feeling when you know there is a piece of land that is so much a part of you. I can't think of being in another place or doing another thing and not having my roots in Hot Springs. In other words, I couldn't give it up for any price.

Chuck:

Five years after that first visit I was taking a friend to the hospital in Fairbanks for surgery. I met an old man down the hall in a wheel chair. I wheeled him to the T. V. set at the end of the hall. It turned out he was Pat Hart from Manley Hot Springs. In the small talk, I mentioned that we had been there, really liked the place, and would like to own it. Why I blurted that out, I don't know, it wasn't as though we had a lot of money. Anyway, he told me the owner, Bob Byer, wanted to sell it. I called up Bob Byer as soon as I left the hospital and made a luncheon date with him for that day. Then I called Gladys and she said, "Go ahead." Bob and I had lunch and worked out a deal. That was it.

Bob Byer owned the mail certificate between Fairbanks, Minto, Manley Hot Springs, Tanana and Rampart. He bill-ed his airline as "the biggest little airline." About a year later he sold the certificate to Wien. He's really a nice guy. He's still flying out of the Seattle area which is where he lives.

The property we purchased was the original 278 acre Karshner homestead. It not only has the hot springs on it, but cold springs as well. Our plans for the property were mostly greenhouse ideas for growing tomatoes. Before we bought this place, I had built a small greenhouse in the College area using polyethylene. We didn't have much of an idea about making it into a resort, which of course we haven't. There was also a bathhouse on the property which we still maintain and make available to the public.

We were really quite fortunate to get the hot springs. There was an executive order in 1912 that withdrew medicinal springs from public entry. There was dispute whether or not some hot springs were medicinal. That was one of the arguments that was used to secure the patent here — that these were not medicinal hot springs because of the low mineral content in the water.

It's funny, on the letterhead of Frank Manley's hotel was that the waters would supposedly cure liver ailments and other things. Frank Manley had a working agreement with

J.F. Karshner, original owner of the hot springs, circa 1907.

Karshner who owned the hot springs. It was a violation of the terms of the homestead act for such an arrangement to be made. Frank Manley didn't have his hotel in operation all that long. He closed it in 1911 or 1912 and in 1913 it burned down. That arrangement was one of the problems in getting patent to the homestead. Ultimately, the patent was issued to the widow of Karshner, Cordelia. About 1918 or 1920, Congress passed an act that withdrew all hot springs from public entry unless they had been under ownership prior to the act.

Hot Springs

This area has quite a history as a mining town. As a matter of fact, there were several thousand people around here in the early 1900's, that's if you count Tofty and Woodchopper and some of the other outlying areas. That's really quite difficult to imagine now in a quiet little town that has about seventy residents in the winter.

Incidentally, Manley as a generic term for the town is not very precise. Until 1957 or '58, the official name here was just Hot Springs. It was on the post office — Hot Springs. It was called Baker Hot Springs on the oldest maps. The Commissioner in his capacity as postmaster engineered the name change from Hot Springs to Manley Hot Springs. I suppose that was due to the fact that a lot of mail was missent to Hot Springs, Arkansas.

More recently, people have dropped the Hot Springs to speak of Manley. That bothers me to a degree. I like to see the identification as Manley Hot Springs rather than Manley. It bothered Pete Johnson. He exploded when he heard the name was to be changed to Manley Hot Springs. "Named for a horse thief!" he says.

The Commissioner had quite a bit of jurisdiction here. He was responsible for swearing people in to be deputized in case there was a crime committed in the area. He was the welfare agent and was responsible for recording. He was

Hot Springs hotel and bridge over Hot Springs Slough, circa 1910.

also a trial judge in certain cases such as game violations. The Hot Springs Recording District was about halfway between here and Rampart in one direction. It went to Fish Lake towards the Tanana direction and I'm not really sure how far up the Kantishna or towards Livengood. I presume it was initially established to record the many mining claims in the area.

Tex Browning was the Commissioner in Prohibition days. During that time there was a telephone system connected with the creeks. It was part of the old Alaska Communication System between Nome and Fairbanks. We heard stories that during Prohibition when an agent was being sent here to make a bust, a contact would call up Mrs. Brentlinger who was living with Tex Browning. That way the local bootleggers would be tipped off.

I don't know, but I've heard nobody was ever pinched here for bootlegging and there were quite a few moonshining and bootlegging operations. There are still two stills here that I know of. Stanley Dayo and Hubbard have part of one. Hubbard uses a large copper vat for his household water storage. Anyway, Gus Benson was the Commissioner for years after Tex Browning, until '69 or '70, when the recording office was moved to Fairbanks. He continued as postmaster, but was soon followed by Rose DeLima. And, of course, now Bob Lee is the postmaster.

Photographs from the University of Alaska show Hot Springs as quite a different looking place in the early 1900's. Much of the area was cleared

The Karshner's hot springs homestead, circa 1910.

at that time, so what you see now is mostly second growth. There was a stable here and Frank Manley's hotel rented horses. Tim Willard had a fox farm. And much of this homestead was farmed. There were cows here in those days and pig pens and chicken coops in the little valley between the present bathhouse and the greenhouse. A large portion of the hillside was cleared and farmed. You can still see furrows in the hillside. I don't know how many acres were involved. I presume that the area across the road on the flats was cleared and farmed. There had to be quite a number of acres cleared and cultivated in order to meet the requirements of the Homestead Act. Karshner produced a healthy number of potatoes for people in the area. But much of what was cleared and cultivated is in second tree growth now.

The Move in '56

The year of '56, was the big flood. Of course, we didn't get here until the flood was over because we came in the last part of May. The flood occurred a couple of weeks before that. When we arrived the bridge was gone so we ferried back and forth across the slough from the airport to the property.

The only way we could get into Hot Springs was fly. The riverboats didn't carry passengers and there was no road between Livengood and Eureka. The road didn't come until three years later. So your only transportation was flying. In those days we did have a bush pilot stationed here.

Tony Lanning hauling firewood, circa 1961.

Frank Jones was the pilot then. Cy Hetherington later took over and expanded the business.

The winter of '56, there was a population of fifteen at Hot Springs. It was old timers and childless couples. There was just the Lanning family with small children. Since Hot Springs didn't have a school, families would leave as soon as their children reached school age. The N. C. Store manager had a teenage daughter they were teaching on correspondence, but they closed down the store that year due to the damage of the flood and lack of business.

Gus Benson was the Commissioner as well as postmaster. Lloyd and Jean Hubbard had the roadhouse. The Clements moved here in '56 also and built that little cabin the Gurtlers have. Some years later they built the large cabin on the property. Stanley Dayo was living here and Bob Kemp was working for the Bureau of Mines. And then there were others who were miners or had been miners. The Pringles, the Lannings, and Pete Johnson, most of them were older people. The Strandbergs bought an acre from Byers before we bought the place, otherwise the original homestead was intact.

The homestead itself didn't look all that different from what it is now. Our present home, of course, wasn't here at the time. There was a five-room log cabin at the bottom of the hill near the old school cabin. The original homestead building which was used as a barn stood across from where the bath is. When we took those buildings down, you could tell from the many layers of wallpaper that they had been lived in a good length of time. There was a small greenhouse attached to the old cabin, but most of the glass was broken out of it.

Many of the cabins around town then are still standing today. And there are probably three or four times as many cabins in the community today. Since '58, there has been a steady increase in population and buildings. I'm pleased to say there are a lot more young people around now too.

During our 27 year involvement with Manley the character has changed three or four times. When we first came here it was primarily old miners and childless couples, which then changed to a few families with children when the school started. Then a number of young people in their early 20's moved in. It wasn't long before the population became as it is now — young couples with children who are staying and raising families.

Gladys:

When people used to ask how life was in Hot Springs in contrast to Fairbanks, I would say the biggest adjustment was trying to plan ahead for family needs. You had to order food in bulk because it was too expensive to fly it in. We ordered food from

L-R: Jeanie and Carol Lee Blackburn, Hazel Dayo, Diane Dart, 1959.

1976, Gladys Dart with Albert George who she describes as, "A naturalist, philosopher and farmer. A very gentle soul."

Visitors from Nenana, Tanana, Minto and Rampart in Manley for Steve Bredeman's potlatch at the home of Judy Woods, 1982. Standing in the center L-R: Sabie Gurtler, Elvie Burk, Maudry Sommers, Josephine Roberts with granddaughter, Annie Titus. Sitting: Rosie Davie, Matilda Titus.

Seattle Commission House one year in advance which would come in by barge. The other concern I had as a mother of three small children was how to handle medical emergencies with them. That always did hang heavy over my head. What would happen if there would be a medical emergency and a pilot would not be able to take off? We were fortunate to never be confronted with such a situation.

People who lived in cities or more populated areas often said, "What do you do living out in a small place? What do you do with all your time?" I generally gave a very noncommital answer, but there hasn't been a winter yet long enough that I have been able to do all those things that I'd put aside "until winter comes." You know, things for pleasure like sculpting or bead work or skin sewing. Things I don't like to do in the summer because I want to spend all that time outside or with the greenhouses. So you wait, you put it aside until wintertime.

Of course, in the winter teaching took up my time. I mentioned that Chuck would do almost one hundred percent of the cooking, well, that was cooking of the meals. On weekends, I used to do the baking and the washing. So you see there really hasn't been time to do more than staying of top of things. And we haven't had to haul in wood each day or any of the other chores that most people with wood stoves have to worry about. Except for the coldest days which amounts to just a couple of weeks, we rely solely on the hot springs for the heating of our home.

Living in a small town like Hot Springs you tend to get involved in things as a community as a whole. We would have fund raising activities for certain things like our weekly movies, that is something we've planned and worked on since 1956. And much of your entertainment would revolve around dinner parties. More recently we've gotten a T. V. station so that's changed the entertainment a small amount, I suppose.

I have never once felt lonely or lonesome in Hot Springs. Summers we have a lot of people in and out of the house all the time. It's not that common for us to sit down and have supper alone together. In fact, I remember Chuck saying once, "Do you realize that we're going to have supper alone together this evening?" It was midafternoon and I told him it may be a little early in the day to say that. Before supper was over that night we had fed thirteen. Of course, it wasn't such a large number everyday, but we did have a lot of unplanned company. We really looked foward to that in the summer. By the time falltime came around, I was glad for the road closing and things quieting down to just the people who lived there year round. And come next spring I was looking foward to the company again. It kind of balanced out well that way.

Outdoors with Berries and Bears

Gladys:

I've never hunted. My husband is not a hunter either. In the twenty-three years that we've been here he shot one moose and I think he's even sorry he did that. He would prefer to shoot with a camera. I used to love to go out snowshoeing or go out into the woods. If I do something like that I just roam on the property since it's 278 acres and there's a lot to see. But if I did go out hiking, it was usually with some purpose in mind.

Mary Clements who was quite an artist and I had some things in common and the diamond willow was one of them. We used to spend hours hiking and looking for diamond willow to carve on. And in the fall, berry picking time is very much a ritual with me. I feel like I've really been denied something each year if I don't get out at berry picking time. Mary and I used to have our little private hidden patches that we never told anybody about. We would take her little boat or canoe and spend the whole day out down the slough. That used to be an annual thing.

Barbara Strandberg who comes here every summer is also someone I like to go out berry picking with. It's more than just berry picking, you know.

You're doing something very useful, collecting berries for the winter jams, jellies and freezing. But it's also something we enjoy very much. I like to spend that time with people who enjoy it as much as I do.

Something that often seems to go along with berry picking is thinking about bears. So I'll tell my story. The first time I told it, I could tell the story in three minutes. Now, it takes me about forty-five. Somebody asked me how big that bear was and I said, "Oh, it must have been at least as big as an elephant!"

This was in the summer of '63, and there were any number of experiences with bears. A lot of strange things were happening and it still is a point of curiosity with me because I don't know what would have caused them to behave the way they did. I never heard any explanation for it. They couldn't have been starving because there were a lot of berries that year.

They just did not scare away like they normally do. Certain noises like tin cans and dogs are supposed to be able to scare them away. Instead of being scared they would turn around and attack instead. If my memory serves me correct, within a mile and a half radius of our town they killed either twenty-six or twenty-nine bears that summer.

Well, on the particular day of my story, I went up on our hill to pick wild strawberries which were just beautiful that summer. We've never had our wild strawberries that good since, or before.

I should explain, Chuck and the two boys happened to be in Fairbanks at the time and Diane and I were at home. The day before I went up the hill to pick berries, I asked Bill Burk who was working on the road to show me how to use Chuck's 300 Savage because it had been so many years since I shot it that I didn't know how to handle it. He said he would be there to help me after work that evening.

I had forgotten about a previous arrangement Diane and I had made with Lee Gardner who was suffering from muscular dystrophy and lived on a houseboat on the slough. He had asked Diane and me to go down on the slough with him and to be his legs for him to check how a blueberry patch was.

When Bill Burk came, I said, "I don't have time to go out and shoot the gun with you. Just tell me how to load it and unload it." Which he did and that was it.

So, as I said, the next day I went up to pick these wonderful strawberries. I went off alone and left Diane at the house to play with Linda Roberts.

I was picking the strawberries on the slope right behind the greenhouse. It's a very steep slope and I was about ten feet from the edge. All of a sudden I had this feeling that someone was close by. I stopped picking and tensed. I turned around and right at the edge of that slope less than ten feet from me was that bear. I don't know if I smelled him or what. All I remember was saying to myself, "If you yell at them or hit a metal can, they'll go away."

I pounded against this coffee can that I was picking the berries in and yelled at the top of my voice. Afterwards I realized that instead of screaming like a lady should, when I screamed it came out in one hoarse voice. The bear just stood and stared at me. It didn't move at all while I was doing this. I panicked.

I spotted one large birch tree standing all by itself twenty feet away in the opposite direction. All I could think of was that I can run faster than that bear around the tree. that will slow him up and then I'll make a dash for the greenhouse. I started running toward the tree and as I looked back he was chasing me. I was running as fast as I could and then I reached the edge of that slope. I hit a soft spot and tumbled. The berries went into the air and all I could see as I went down were these little red dots floating around in the air all around me. My glasses fell off and broke. As I picked myself up I looked up and there was the bear sitting on its haunches on the edge of the slope. I dashed for the greenhouse.

I went way inside the greenhouse. After calming myself, I went to the door and didn't see the bear so I ran for the house. When I got there I told the girls the bear had chased me. You know, all I could think of was those berries. I lost about two quarts of real nice ones. Then I got mad and told the girls, "We're going to go right back up there and pick some more berries. I'll take the gun up there and kill it if I see it." We went right back up but the bear never showed up.

It started to rain that afternoon, one of those hard rains that you have on a hot summer afternoon. Diane and I went down to the bath. We came back up to the house and Diane was telling me a creative story that she had thought of. We were sitting there in robes and wet hair. All of a sudden we both stopped and turned around. We could see through the clear plastic walls. There was the bear in our front yard!

We had a malemute dog and the bear went for him. The two of them took off into the woods right across our yard. I grabbed the gun and we went out. It was going down the hill toward the bathhouse and right up the steep slope towards Strandbergs. I said, "We're going to get it."

We walked up the hill and Diane said, "There he is! He's on his haunches." I suppose I started to panic again. Not even thinking all I did was go at that bear. I just took up my gun without aiming and shot. It was just ridiculous. There we were on a rainy day, in robes and slippers and wet hair. And I'm jumping off the ground with my robe wide open and rifle at my hip pointing towards the bear. Utterly stupid. Diane said she looked at me and the whole scene was so funny, she couldn't help but laugh.

As we headed back towards the house, we saw the bear going across the valley where Karshner Creek runs. Then I had the sense to go ahead and take aim at that bear. He was probably three or four hundred feet away when I shot. "Oh, Diane, I missed it by a mile."

Diane Dart at home, 1961.

It just took off across the creek and into some ferns that were four or five feet high. We went back up to the house.

Horace Roberts, Linda's dad, bless his heart, went to the spot where I had first seen the bear and waited there every morning and evening. He told me, "You know, I think you got that bear. It would have been back. I think you hurt it." Then I felt horrible. I had visions of this wounded bear.

We got serious and the ladies in town got together and all went out to the gravel pit and did some serious target shooting. By that time I had a terrible feeling all the time. When I'd go up to the greenhouse to work I'd carry my gun with me. And all those shadows were becoming bears. I knew that I should straighten my line of thinking, but I couldn't help it. When I'd go around the corner of a house, I'd look first to be sure that a bear wouldn't be coming. But our shooting was better and I felt more comfortable about that anyway.

A week passed and by this time the boys had come home. I was having trouble with the pipes that were running to the bathhouse and had to find where they had broken apart. I was walking up the creek barefoot checking each joint. Once as I bent over, I glanced sideways into the ferns and I saw this black shadow again. I thought, "Oh my god! That bear." I just dropped the pipes and ran to where the boys were playing at Strandbergs. All I could say was, "Come and see what I see. I can't wait, come and see what I see." They ran ahead of me and I yelled to them where to look. They jumped across the creek spread the ferns apart and there was the bear. I had gotten it with one shot. Between the hot summer days and the rain that bear was just a horrible stench.

We decided to bury him right there. Arnold Griese happened to come by for a bath at that time so he did his neighborly duty and dug the hole. Jim wanted to put a white cross there as a monument for the bear. I'm sorry he didn't do that because we'd know exactly where he was buried today. And that's my bear story.

Actually, it was a week later that Bill Strandberg was killed at the mine over a hill in Tofty. If it would have been the other way around and I had met that bear a week after Bill's tragedy, I would have died of a heart attack right there. It was a horrible situation because he was at the mine alone and the bear had partially eaten him by the time he was found. The combination of that experience and a couple others in town totally changed my opinion about bears. I have a good feeling when somebody says that they've shot a bear. I can't help feeling that way now.

I had horrible nightmares all that summer because Chuck was away working construction and I was alone at the house with the three children. After that, Barbara Strandberg and I had bears come between our houses and she was home alone with her youngest son too. When we would visit each other we'd carry guns. That fall we moved to Fairbanks because the children had reached junior high age.

A few times after that incident things happened that brought back the feeling or smell of being chased by that bear and I've panicked. A few summers ago we had a garden at the bottom of that slope. Liza and I were working there. Well, all of a sudden we heard this noise of an animal crashing through the brush. It was thirteen years since that bear incident, but I panicked, threw that hoe I had in my hand and ran about fifty feet before I realized what I had done. I stood there trying to calm myself and said, "What am I doing?" As we stood there, here comes Liza's dog, Slug, out of the woods. She had been trained not to come up to the greenhouse so she had walked all the way around through the woods and came through the back way to see Liza.

I've had a lot of people tell me the mistake I made with that bear was in running away from it. They said I should have run toward it to scare it away. I'm sure they're right and it works that way most of the time. But I'm also sure with only ten feet between us, if I had run toward it I would never have had the chance to turn away again. I would never have gotten away. Not the way the bears acted that summer.

Manley Hot Springs in the '80's

Chuck:

I think this is a nice quiet little place to live now. I would like to see it remain kind of low key with no great amount of commercialism. I'm not opposed to anybody having a good streak of luck, but I wouldn't welcome the idea of a mineral deposit that would have a mine here with four or five hundred miners involved. That would alter the community to a degree that I don't feel would be very good. It would be good for those that wanted to ring the cash register, but that's about it. I think most people living here want to get away from that sort of thing. It's a shame that so many people have to go away for short periods to make a living. On the other hand, I think that's the sacrifice many people are willing to make in order to live in such a nice town.

There are some jobs that open up here every once in a while. The only full-time, year round work is the postmaster's job. The three highway department positions are for a six-month period. The school teacher has a nine month position and now that Gladys and Damaris split the school year, it's only four and a half months each. The gold mines operate about six months and there is work for some there. There's some fishing and work at the fish processing plants of J. L. Wood and Bill Taylor. Sometimes an exploration crew comes in here and will hire a few people. Some people are self-employed, but they have small operations that don't hire outside of the family.

The Dart's hot springs bathhouse through frost covered trees.

I think various people here have been supportive of some of the individuals that have arrived here and stayed over the years. The boys that came up from Kansas City directly from graduating have done pretty well. That was Steve Bredeman, Barry Shockley and Dennis Hollingsworth.

It's certainly a place that people become attracted to and want to come back. It just happens that a lot of people who come here can't make a living. The land situation is also a problem. There just isn't any land available to most people who would like to build a home here. It's also tough to make a living trapping. There's very little fur around here. The most activity here revolves around gold mining, with the price of gold up there are quite a few people staking claims.

I don't forsee any great changes here. Granted there have been a few changes in the past few years. I mentioned the fish processing plants a while ago. I certainly hadn't imagined an operation that would be processing fish for shipment, not to mention preparing salmon eggs for export to Japan.

And through the efforts of Jerry Hook we now have telephone service and television. The town raised $1,500 and I'm not sure what Jerry raised through the Geophysical Institute. He and Jack Neubauer with his cat laid cable to the site up on the hill where the translator is. The town now receives one public broadcasting channel which carries some very good programs. I don't know how the coming of television has changed the relating of people amongst themselves. People still get together

Aerial of "downtown" Manley Hot Springs, 1982. The largest group of houses are situated between the Hot Springs Slough and the runway.

quite a bit and socialize.

Gladys:

I don't see any great changes coming about either. I do believe the 1991 deadline for the Native Land claims Act is of great importance to the Native people here. And, of course, Manley Hot Springs is a Native Village under the Act. I think there is an urgency with the Natives to be educated by that deadline so they will realize the value of their inheritance and be ready to handle the responsibility. It's really a short time until they will be receiving title to their lands. It's possible that the Bean Ridge Corporation could alter the employment picture if they so chose at that time.

Anyway, in the next five or ten years I don't see any rapid growth for Hot Springs. In all modesty, you have to recognize that development of the hot springs is part of the key to what could suddenly change the town. I can't see it happening under the Darts. But, if there should be a sudden change in ownership, for instance a big corporation that would develop the property and town into a tourist attraction, that could alter the town considerably. And I really can't see that happening under any of the Darts.

I think all three of the children have a very strong feeling about our property. They all have part of the property and have built homes or are planning to. They would spend all of their time here if they could. About the only thing that takes them away is economics. They need to leave to make money and then they come back. I believe they sacrifice to be here. But I do feel they grew up in an ideal place. No matter what development they might decide on when it's their decision to make, I'm glad their childhood was spent the way it was.

Greenhouses

Chuck:

The changes we have planned for the hot springs area itself is a new bathhouse which is under construction at present. The new bathhouse will be a series of pools with some portable partitions and various plants growing. The present bath can only accommodate one party of bathers at a time and in the summer we have to turn people away due to the great demand. We make reservations for people and it's not uncommon to have that list filled for the day by noon time. I do hope to remedy that situation soon.

Other plans include more greenhouses. The existing greenhouse is 72 feet wide and 120 feet long. I have plans to extend that 48 feet in length. There are other ideas for additional greenhouses besides, but that is in the future.

Presently we grow tomatoes, eggplant, and green peppers which we start the first of February. The melons and cucumbers are started a bit later. We have been getting the others into the ground during the last week in March and the first week in April. Now that we've buried polyethylene pipes underground with hot water running through, we may be able to get things in the ground a little sooner with the added warm soil temperature.

We've also grown a few flowers and produced some bedding plants, plants to be transplanted in the outdoor gardens later in the year. We did have some grapes that weren't very successful. We've even stuck a couple of papayas in the ground. They got about ten inches high and then died. I really doubt that they'll ever be brought to production because of time and lighting. I do grow a number of orchids, however, which I really prize. I'm sure I'll keep experimenting with different plants. As far as real quantities, it is the tomato we produce the most of. We sell quite a few tomatoes locally. As you might guess, we spend most of our time during the summer with the greenhouse.

Chuck pulling out greenhouse tomato plants at the end of the growing season, October 1982.

Photo by Yvonne Yarber

Gladys and Chuck during spring tomato transplanting in their greenhouse, April 1983.

Chuck watering tomato starts in the greenhouse, March 1983.

Chuck in the greenhouse.

Top of Roughtop, looking south towards Bean Ridge, winter 1983. L-R: John Dart, Heidi Heidtke, Dennis Hollingsworth.

John Dart making a marten poleset on his trapline behind Roughtop Mountain, 1983.

Jim Dart back from the trapline with a wolf, 1983.

John Dart at the Manley Spring Carnival sno-go race, March 1982.

Jim Dart operating "Mahalia", summer '83.

Cars being moved to high ground via the downtown road in Manley Hot Springs during the spring flood of '82.

The old bridge abutment on the slough the year before the ice took it out, 1982.

Photo by Yvonne Yarber

Visitors from Minto singing at Steve Bredeman's potlatch while young Harvey Titus looks on. L-R: Daisy Hetherington, Sarah Silas, Sirosky Charlie, Matthew Titus, Dorothy Titus, Evelyn Alexander.

1983 school Christmas performance for the Manley community. L-R: Amy Evans, Michelle Woods, Glenn Evans, Patrice Dade, Mark Evans, Derrick Joiner as Santa, Heather Dade. Front row: Sean Carney, Marilynn Woods, Charles Woods, Kris Shockley, Patrick Hook.

Fourth of July 1981 in the park, 4:00 a.m., Frank Gurtler on guitar and Arvin Kangas on kazoo.

Gladys Dart and Sally Hudson in their fine winter parkas, circa 1970's.

Charlie Pearson on sax and Curt Madison on guitar at John and Liza's, February 1983.

Index

Frost covered front door of the Dart's hot springs bathhouse.

The *Yukon-Koyukuk Biography* Series

Available from Spirit Mountain Press

Edgar Kallands - Kaltag	**$6.95**
Josephine Roberts - Tanana	**$6.95**
Billy McCarty - Ruby	**$6.95**
Simeon Mountain - Nulato	**$8.95**
Altona Brown - Ruby	**$14.95**

Coming Soon:

Goodwin Semaken - Kaltag

Henry Ekada - Nulato

Peter John - Minto

Al Wright - Minto

Martha Joe - Nulato

POSTAGE AND HANDLING

Add $1.00 for first book, 50ᶜ for each additional book. Orders of 10 or more, shipping will be billed.

Send order to:

Spirit Mountain Press

P.O. Box 1214   **Fairbanks, Alaska 99707**

Dart's Family Tree

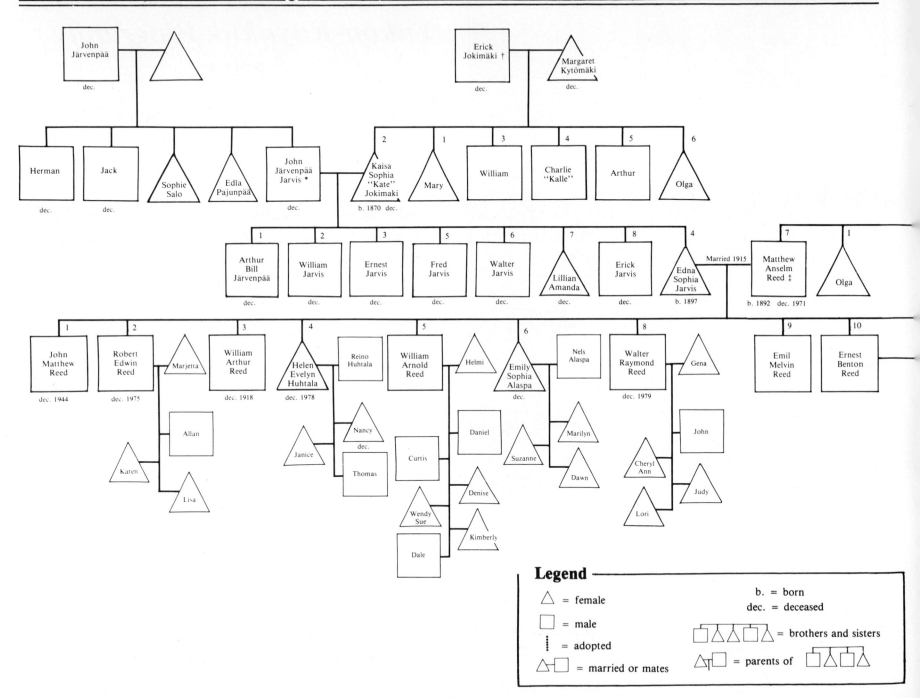

Legend

△ = female

□ = male

⋮ = adopted

△—□ = married or mates

b. = born

dec. = deceased

□△△□△ = brothers and sisters

△⊤□ = parents of □△△△